# THE END OF THE WEST

The Public Square Book Series

Princeton University Press
Ruth O'Brien, Series Editor

# THE END OF THE WEST
## THE ONCE AND FUTURE EUROPE

## DAVID MARQUAND

PRINCETON UNIVERSITY PRESS

PRINCETON AND OXFORD

Copyright © 2011 by David Marquand
Requests for permission to reproduce material from this work should be
sent to Permissions, Princeton University Press
Published by Princeton University Press, 41 William Street,
Princeton, New Jersey 08540
In the United Kingdom: Princeton University Press, 6 Oxford Street,
Woodstock, Oxfordshire OX20 1TW

press.princeton.edu

Jacket photo: Constantine Manos, Man Reading Newspaper,
Chania, Crete, 1962, from A Greek Portfolio. © Costa Manos/Magnum.

All Rights Reserved

Library of Congress Cataloging-in-Publication Data
Marquand, David.
The end of the West : the once and future Europe / David Marquand.
p.   cm. — (The public square book series)
Includes bibliographical references and index.
ISBN 978-0-691-14159-6 (hardcover : acid-free paper)  1.  European Union
countries—Politics and government—21st century. 2.  Europe—Politics and
government—21st century.  I. Title.
JN30.M3536 2011
320.94—dc22      2010046141

British Library Cataloging-in-Publication Data is available

This book has been composed in Minion Pro
Printed on acid-free paper. ∞

Printed in the UK by CPI William Clowes Beccles NR34 7TL

1  3  5  7  9  10  8  6  4  2

To the memory of
*Nina Fishman and Ghita Ionescu,*
*dear friends and staunch Europeans*

———⋙•⋘———

# CONTENTS

# FOREWORD

*Ruth O'Brien*

—————⟫◆⟪—————

TEACHING AMERICAN POLITICS TO Ph.D. students in the United States is always an engaging experience. Understanding how the Constitutional Convention concocted the so-called three-fifths compromise, in which a slave embodied this ratio to reconcile representation between the Southern agrarian slave states and the Northern mercantile free states, leads to lively discussions. Yet addressing the more recent workings of governance is a good way to kill any discussion. By the time we reach federalism, my students begin squirming. Former Supreme Court Chief Justice William Rehnquist's "new federalism" doctrine fires up my students much less than Thomas Jefferson, John Marshall, and James Madison.

In *The End of the West*, David Marquand does not face this disjunction between the origins and governance. In this, the European Project's sixtieth anniversary year, Marquand provides near perfect pitch, portraying the "unmistakable federalist direction" that defines the EU's governance structure that is "unfolding no matter what" alongside unraveling its very complicated origins.

To do so, Marquand asks, who were the European Union's founding fathers? Why is there no James Madison leading elevated discussions about virtue and liberty? Lacking a Madison, let alone a *Federalist Papers*, Marquand provides us with a masterly book that constitutes a different kind of call to action. This book encourages European peoples and politicians to unpack, critically analyze, and ponder the intersecting and interconnecting mazes and webs of ambiguities, contradictions, and outright evasions underlying the European Project, along with the EU's emergence and transformation in real time.

Marquand makes us face some "sobering facts." As the European Project evolved into a quasi-federalist system of governance, its "success" stemmed from the post–World War II history of a continent soaked "in blood and shame" seeking to avoid yet another multinational war. Yet, as the prospect of such a catastrophe faded, the European Project fell prey to some careerism and horse-trading even though some visionary leaders followed some of its focused and pragmatic founders.

In pairings, Marquand discusses ethnicity and identity, EU governance and authority, and civilization and territory. Having expanded more than fourfold from the original six to twenty-seven member states, stretching geographically and culturally from Ireland to Turkey, how much farther are they going? Where does Europe begin and end? Being "non-ethnic and implicitly anti-ethnic," the European Project may have "expelled ethnicity through door" only to find it has now come in through an EU "window."

Marquand finds it ironic that just as the EU has enhanced its governance and authority, the member states' publics participate less and less in electing their members of the European Parliament, despite far-right national parties' stirring up resentment of "the ultra-rich, of unemployment and insecurity, of the left intelligentsia, of the political class, of immigrants, and of the EU itself." In the face of all this, along with stresses like immigration, terrorism, and the global financial crisis, can the label "European" command any allegiance, except as a convenient euphemism for Germans traveling abroad? Might the design of Europe's bold framers someday face a sectional crisis?

Marquand warns us that the languages of *realpolitik* and *raison d'état*, no matter how successful, never come out of a cultural vacuum. Now Marquand fills that vacuum with a grand narrative having the necessary historical sweep. "All lies in the past," he points out poignantly. Differentiating between medieval Judaeophobia and the nineteenth- and twentieth-century anti-Semitism that led to the Holocaust, Marquand will have readers pondering: Is the Muslim question reminiscent of the Jewish Question? Or is this a "clash of civilizations" associated with the tribal democracy that fed Judaeophobia? As the EU expands, can it go beyond the politics of tolerance and multiculturalism and govern on the basis of difference and diversity?

Marquand gives his readers a challenge. While the German Constitutional Court upheld the Lisbon Treaty, reinforcing a type of constitutionalism that circumvented negative national referendums in France, the Netherlands, and Ireland, it left the member states and their peoples two caveats to chew on like a ship's hardtack and start trying to resolve. First, the Court ruled, there is "no uniform European people" capable of expressing its majority will. And second, European decision making does not take "due account of equality." Small nations have more weight than big ones. Hence, a "structural democratic deficit" has long plagued the EU.

I won't spoil the ending by exposing how Marquand proposes to resolve these two caveats. Nor will I diminish the way he unfurls the EU's breathtaking opportunities and accomplishments, such as anti-discrimination rights that aren't just civil but part of the body of human rights, or the way so much member-state legislation, as in Ireland, has been inspired by actions of the EU. The European Court of Justice—modeled consciously after the U.S. Supreme Court, Marquand reminds us—renders decisions that bind national courts and the member states' national governments, sometimes, in suits that can be filed by individual citizens, ordering governments to change unjust laws and public policies.

Most of all, *The End of the West* shows my students why they should struggle harder. Neither they nor their European counterparts, in universities and on the streets, can afford to be free from a self-conscious understanding that the EU's present is part of the past, even as it represents the future. Issues of ethnicity, identity, territory, and civilization are essential for our understanding of the EU and, by comparison, the United States; and *The End of the West* will generate great discussion on all these points, making it a thoroughly worthy contribution to the Public Square.

# ACKNOWLEDGMENTS

THIS BOOK COULD NOT HAVE BEEN written without help, advice, moral support, and, in some cases, inspiration from a wide variety of people in several different countries. I have lectured or presented papers on the themes of the book at the Robert Schuman Centre at the European University Institute in Florence, the Centre for Federal Studies at the University of Kent, the Centre for European Studies at the Jagiellonian University in Krakow, the University of Rostov-on-Don, the Politics Department at Swansea University, Mansfield College Oxford, the India International Centre in Delhi, and the Complutense University in Madrid. Warm thanks to all these institutions for their kindness and hospitality, and to my audiences at these events for their spirited questions and thought-provoking feedback. Warm thanks too to Paul Flather, secretary general of the Europaeum network of European universities, for facilitating my visits to the Jagiellonian and Complutense universities, and to Vasantha and Suresh Bharucha for helping to secure temporary membership of the lively and welcoming India International Centre for my wife and me, and for enabling us both to sing for our suppers at that splendid institution.

I have older debts to acknowledge as well. I became a committed supporter of the European project as a backbench Labour Member of Parliament, more than forty years ago. High on the list of my European mentors were Roy Jenkins, future president of the European Commission; Lilo Milch-sach, the founder and chatelaine of the annual Anglo-German conferences at Königswinter; John Mackintosh, my brilliant and eloquent parliamentary colleague; and John Pinder, indefatigable champion of federalism both then and now. All of these helped to make me a European of the heart as well as of the head. Though they played no direct part in the making of this book, their influence shines through it, and I take this opportunity to acknowledge my debt to them. Later, the experience of working in the European Commission played a crucial part in my European education, as did my membership of the Board of Trustees of the Aspen Institute, Berlin. I learned even more from innumerable conversations with two dear friends: Ghita Ionescu, analyst and prophet of transnational interdependence and its implications for European integration; and Nina Fishman, insightful student of contemporary European social democracy and indomitable champion of the European cause. This book is dedicated to their memory.

At an early stage in working on this book, I enjoyed the welcoming hospitality of Dick and Irène Leonard, and profited from Dick's wise guidance through the highways and byways of the Brussels Euro-village. I also profited greatly from conversations with Robert Cooper, Michael Emerson, Roger Liddle, and Antonio Missiroli. To all of these warm thanks. My inspirational editor, Brigitta van Rheinberg, has been a delight to work with; my agent, Anthony Goff, has been an unfailing source of moral support; and my copyeditor, Joan Gieseke, has blended sensitivity and rigor with extraordinary skill. The three anonymous reviewers of my original proposal, and their three equally anonymous successors who commented on the final draft of my manuscript, helped me to correct mistakes of logic and fact and to hone my argument. I am hugely indebted to all of these—and indeed to everyone else at Princeton University Press who played a part in the production of this book. Most of all, I am indebted to my wife, Judith—not just for her unfailing enthusiasm, but for her critical acumen and creative imagination. It goes without saying that any remaining flaws are my own.

# THE END OF THE WEST

# -I-

## PROLOGUE

—————◈—————

Oh, East is East, and West is West, and never the twain shall meet,
Till Earth and Sky stand presently at God's great judgement seat;
But there is neither East nor West, Border, nor Breed, nor Birth,
When two strong men stand face to face, tho' they come from the
ends of the earth!
　　　　　　—Rudyard Kipling, "The Ballad of East and West," 1889

The future of Western political theory will be decided outside the West.
　　　　　　—Sunil Khilnani, *The Idea of India*, 2003

FOR CENTURIES, THE THEME OF Kipling's "Ballad of East and West" has woven in and out of Western imaginations like a blood-stained thread. It first appeared in the fifth century BCE, when the small and turbulent city-states of ancient Greece fought off the vast Persian Empire to the east. Nearly two and a half millennia later, it provided the rhetorical underpinning for the Atlantic Alliance. After the fall of the Berlin Wall, it surfaced in Francis Fukuyama's notorious claim that Western democracy had become the "final form of human government." At the start of the twenty-first century, it reverberated through George W. Bush's depiction of the so-called war on terror as a battle between the civilized and the uncivilized.

1

It is, in fact, an ever-ready rhetorical maid-of-all-work. It has been pressed into service by innumerable political leaders searching for perorations and has lurked in the psyches of a variety of foreign policy intellectuals. To mention only a few examples, the neoconservative American commentator Robert Kagan, the British diplomat and European civil servant Robert Cooper, and the American historian and legal theorist Philip Bobbitt differ in much. But they have all shared the assumption that there is a distinct, identifiable place called "the West," whose uniquely precious values are under threat from other quarters of the globe.[1] Yet in the fluid world of the twenty-first century—a world where the American president is the son of a black Kenyan who started as a goatherd, where India is easily the most populous democracy, where the U.S. debt to China stands at $800 billion, and where the Atlantic Alliance is riven with doubts—that assumption is less a guide to understanding than a semantic comfort blanket. And, as often happens to comfort blankets, it has grown threadbare with use.

Then why do so many people cling to it? Why does Kipling's drumbeat still reverberate today? The answer is that his antimony of "West" versus "East" encapsulates one of the most venerable narratives—and most cherished myths—of the North Atlantic world. Its emotional essence has changed very little in the last twenty-five hundred years. Ancient Greeks, fighting in the Persian wars, took it for granted that they stood for civilization against barbarism and for freedom against tyranny. Greeks governed themselves; Persians were governed despotically by tyrannical kings. And where Persian barbarians were slavish, the Scythian barbarians of the steppes beyond the Black Sea were wild, unsettled, and ungovernable. Both were self-evidently inferior to the civilized Greeks. Change a few words, and it might be modern Americans invading Iraq or fighting the Taliban.

2

The Romans inherited these stereotypes from the Greeks, and the early Christians from the Romans. After the rise of Islam, the Church gave them an ominous new gloss: "eastern" Muslims were infidels who desecrated the Holy Land and deserved to be put to the sword. The most horrifying example of this mind-set came in 1099, when Christian crusaders sacked Muslim Jerusalem and went on a rampage that left the streets running ankle deep in blood. (In some places, the blood was said to have been knee-deep.) In the fifteenth century CE, Constantinople, the capital of the Christian Byzantine Empire, fell to the quintessentially "eastern" Ottoman Turks, who pushed far into Europe during the next two centuries. In the "West," the Turks, like the Persians before them, became bywords for cruelty, despotism, and depravity. The great nineteenth-century British Liberal, W. E. Gladstone, was using a well-worn trope when he accused them of indulging in "abominable and bestial lusts" while suppressing a revolt in Bulgaria.[2] (A frequent charge against the Turks was that they had a loathsome propensity for homosexual rape,[3] but whether Gladstone was referring to that is not clear.)

Meanwhile, the Renaissance led "Western" scholars back to the ancient Greek texts. (Ironically, many of them had been preserved and translated by Muslim scholars, whose commentaries on them eventually became part of the European philosophical canon.) These helped to make the language of West versus East, freedom versus despotism, and civilization versus barbarism part of the mental furniture of the educated classes all over Europe. Shimmering on the edge of the imaginative universe of the classically educated elites who governed the continent was a vision of Plato teaching in the Academy, of the Athenian Parthenon, glowing in the attic sun—and of the legendary three hundred Spartan warriors dying gloriously at Thermopylae to hold off a Persian army numbered in tens of thousands.[4]

The long-term effects of the Renaissance went wider still. It spawned an intellectual and cultural revolution that transformed the world. Even at the highest point of Roman grandeur, the Roman Empire was only one of many global power centers. It dominated western Europe, the Balkans, and the Mediterranean, but it never managed to subjugate the once Persian territories east of what is now Iraq. It was outranked in wealth and technological sophistication by India and China; and after the fall of Rome, western Europe sank into impoverished and anarchic mediocrity, relieved only by the astonishingly creative and tolerant civilization of "Moorish"—in other words, Muslim and therefore "eastern"—Spain.[5] In the late sixteenth century, when Europeans were burning heretics at the stake, Akbar, the great Mughal emperor of northern India, used to hold interfaith dialogues between Muslims, Hindus, Christians, Parsees, Jews, and Jains. (Not all Mughal emperors emulated Akbar: in the seventeenth century, the Emperor Aurangzeb was a byword for narrow-minded and puritanical intolerance.)

As late as 1700, the combined GDP of India and China was twice as large as Europe's. Thanks to a mixture of force, fraud, and guile, widening tracts of Indian territory fell under British rule in the second half of the eighteenth century, but the new rulers did not imagine that they were racially or culturally superior to their subjects. They were in India to make money, not to save souls or disseminate "Western" values. Many took Indian concubines, and some married Indian wives; a few converted to Indian faiths.[6] Farther east, the Chinese saw themselves as denizens of a "middle kingdom," sufficient unto itself and ineffably superior to vulgar western barbarians: in 1793, after a famous encounter with a British mission led by Lord George Macartney, the Chinese emperor replied loftily to a British request for trade relations with China: "We have never valued ingenious articles, nor do we have the slightest need of your country's manufactures."[7]

But the indirect impact of the Renaissance—notably, the scientific revolution, a variety of different Enlightenments, the growth of industrial society, and, not least, the establishment of globe-girdling European empires—slowly made Europe the powerhouse and center of the world. By 1913, Europe's share of global GDP was more than twice those of India and China put together. (It was twice that of the United States.)[8] The British Empire covered one-quarter of the earth's land surface; the City of London was the linchpin of the world's first truly global market. The Russian Empire—not fully European, but ruled from its far-western capital in European St. Petersburg—extended from Warsaw in the west to the Pacific Ocean in the east. France ruled vast territories in North and West Africa as well as much of Southeast Asia. Soft power mimicked hard power. French was the language of diplomacy and culture, German of philosophy, and English of political economy. Of the great transformative ideologies of the age, liberalism was a British invention, republicanism a Franco-Italian one, and socialism and nationalism Franco-German ones.

European intellectuals and statesmen imbibed an ever more potent version of the ancient Greek mixture. The utilitarian theorist James Mill—father of the much greater John Stuart Mill—wrote a supposedly authoritative multivolume history of India, without ever visiting the subcontinent or learning any of its languages. In it, he opined that "deceit and perfidy" were the hallmarks of "the Hindu."[9] In one of his most famous poems, Kipling called on the Americans to take up the "white man's burden" in the Philippines, which they had just conquered from Spain. Kipling explained what he meant with brutal clarity:

> Go bind your sons to exile
> To serve your captives' need;
> To wait in heavy harness,
> On fluttered folk and wild—
> Your new-caught, sullen peoples,
> Half devil and half child.

The French-born British Liberal Hilaire Belloc offered a simpler and more cynical interpretation of the imperial vocation:

> Whatever happens, we have got
> The Maxim gun, and they have not.

Not only was Europe the center of the world, but Europeans took it for granted that their "Western" values were predestined victors in a Darwinian struggle for moral and ideological supremacy. Europe was the home of ever-advancing modernity and progress. Its trajectory was a model for humanity. And within Europe, the same mentality prevailed. For the French, France was the heart of the European "west." The Germans were "easterners"—uncouth at best, destructive at worst. For the Germans, these were quintessentially Russian characteristics. The Russians themselves were unsure where they belonged. "Westernizers" tacitly conceded that Russia was "eastern" but hoped it would follow the path taken by progressive, enlightened western Europe. "Slavophiles" rejected the materialism and individualism of the "west," cherished the ancient vision of Moscow as the Third Rome, and believed that Russia should follow a unique, transcendental path of her own. For the British, even the French were at least a shade "eastern": "Wogs," insular Britons used to say, "begin at Calais." (Wogs were "wily oriental gentlemen.") In similar vein, the Austrian statesman Prince Metternich famously declared that "Asia begins at the Landstrasse"—the great highway leading eastward from Vienna into Hungary.

It was not clear where the United States fit in. It was indubitably Western. Like Russia, only more so, it was an offshoot of Europe. The urbane and cultivated gentlemen who founded it belonged to the same civilization as the elites on the European side of the Atlantic. In the nineteenth century, millions of European immigrants, fleeing poverty and oppression and inspired by the American dream of liberty and opportunity, left their homes to settle in the United States, where they helped to remake American civilization. But for other Europeans, the United States was more like Scythia than Greece. American democracy was less a promise than a threat. For Americans themselves, the United States epitomized the West. It was self-governing, freedom loving, democratic, trustworthy, and progressive. It was also a providential, uniquely righteous nation: the "city on a hill," the last best hope of the world's poor and oppressed. Europe, with its bloodthirsty wars, corrupt aristocracies, and cynical wiles, was, as Thomas Jefferson put it, "a field of slaughter"—or as Walt Whitman thought, "a stale and drowsy lair, the lair of slaves."[10] In his farewell address at the end of his presidency, George Washington famously advised his countrymen to steer clear of European entanglements. For more than a century, most of them did so.

Europe's centrality was short-lived. The First World War— the twentieth century's first great European civil war—dealt it a grievous blow. The peace conference that followed the war was held in Paris, the most "European" of all capital cities; the potentates assembled there redrew the maps, not just of Europe, but of the Middle East, large parts of Africa, and even parts of east Asia. However, the chief potentate was the stiff-necked and self-righteous American president, Woodrow Wilson. He arrived in Paris bathed in the delusive aura of a savior, determined to remake the wicked Old World in the virtuous image of the New. Though his fellow country-men returned to their isolationist ways even before he left the White House, the absent United States still loomed on the horizon of European politics—a symbol of hope for some and a portent of danger for others. (So did that other great emblem of ideological redemption, the Soviet Union.)

The Second World War destroyed Europe's central-ity once and for all. In the immediate aftermath of the war, most of continental Europe was devastated, and much of it was traumatized. The death tolls defy imagination—nearly six million Jews, more than seven million Germans, more than two million non-Jewish Poles, more than a million Yu-goslavs, nearly a million Rumanians, and more than twenty million Soviet citizens (not all of them Europeans). Warsaw was systematically torched and dynamited, block by block. Industrial Germany was flattened. Eight and a half square miles of Hamburg were incinerated in a firestorm, caused by Allied bombing. When Germany surrendered uncondi-tionally in May 1945, much of Berlin was a heap of rubble.[11] During the next twenty years, the great European maritime empires disappeared. Kipling's "fluttered folk" became citi-zens of independent states; India, once the brightest jewel in the British Crown, became a great power in its own right, playing an important role in world affairs.

More significant for the long term than the killing and the physical destruction—more significant than even the huge population movements that transformed the ethnic map of eastern and central Europe—was a seismic shift in

8

the balance of European power and in Europe's position in the global order. The war had started in Europe, for European motives driving European states. But it was also lost by Europe, including the nominally victorious Britain. The true winners were Europe's twin offshoots—the Soviet Union and (still more) the United States. The war's most obvious result was to carry both twins from the periphery of the continent to its heart. The ensuing cold war between them shaped its history for nearly half a century. Not only had Europe ceased to be the center of the world; it had become the cockpit of a worldwide struggle for supremacy between two rival visions of human destiny and the good society, incarnated by two non-European superpowers, which towered over their European allies.

But the old rhetoric of "West" and "East," which had helped to structure Europeans' self-understanding since the days of Herodotus and Pericles, survived and prospered. For "westerners," Washington DC became the new Rome, if not quite the new Athens. The Soviet Union, Ronald Reagan's "evil empire," became a cross between Persia and Scythia. The Oder-Neisse line that divided totalitarian Eastern Europe from democratic Western Europe was the new Bosphorus.

The mental map that resulted was curious, to put it mildly. The Japanese, hosts to large American bases, became honorary westerners. After the Communist Party took power in mainland China, the once-Chinese island of Taiwan, then known to most westerners as Formosa, and ruled by the not notably democratic Guomindang party of Chiang-Kai-shek, became another outpost of the "West," as did South Korea. (It is fair to say that Japan, South Korea, and Taiwan *are* west of California.) Turkey, viscerally anti-Russian since the days of Catherine the Great and, as such, a staunch American ally, was now more "Western" than the Communist satellites of

Czechoslovakia and Poland, whose capitals lie far to the west of Istanbul, to say nothing of Ankara, the Turkish capital. Fidel Castro's Cuba was an "eastern" outpost on America's doorstep. Pesky would-be neutrals, like Tito's Yugoslavia, Nasser's Egypt, and Nehru's India, inhabited a cartographic limbo.

But these curiosities hardly mattered. What did matter was that there was a passable fit between the realities of postwar Europe and ancient narratives of "West" and "East." Europe east of the iron curtain was not as homogeneous as "Western" cold warriors imagined. Nor was it as immune to the cultural and intellectual shifts that took place in North America and non-Communist Europe. The 1968 "Prague spring" that seemed, for a magical moment, to portend a humane and liberal form of Communism in Czechoslovakia had something in common with the student revolts that swept through western campuses from California to Berlin. But when all the caveats have been entered, the brute reality is that Soviet power and the Soviet system reigned throughout the Communist satellites of Eastern Europe, with only trivial variations. They were all gray, grim, grubby one-party states, honeycombed with informers and lumbered with hopelessly inefficient and unproductive command economies. In all of them, censorship was omnipresent and heresy-hunting endemic. Everywhere civil associations were colonized by the party-state; everywhere, a culture of mistrust prevailed.

In non-Communist Western Europe, things were more complicated. Until well into the 1980s, the Communist parties of France and Italy enjoyed substantial mass support. Communism had no political purchase in the German Federal Republic, and though Communists had some influence in certain British trade unions, the British Communist Party was a negligible force in parliamentary politics. The political economies of Western Europe were variegated too. The neo-corporatist "social market" economies of the German Federal Republic and its smaller western neighbors were heavily influenced by Catholic social teaching. In France, a tradition of statist economic intervention dating from the seventeenth century spawned a distinctively French form of indicative planning, underpinned by a large nationalized sector. Britain also had a large nationalized sector, but repeated attempts to mimic French-style planning collapsed in failure and recrimination.

However, these were variations on a set of common themes. Four of them stood out. The first and most obvious was that the security of the entire region was underpinned by American power, above all by American nuclear weapons—enabling Europeans to enjoy a moral free ride by courtesy of the American air force. The second was that, partly because American Marshall aid in the early postwar years facilitated an astonishing spurt of economic growth that continued long after American aid ceased to flow, the region was saved for capitalism. Rapid growth took the edge off distributional conflicts and gave organized labor a stake in the success of the capitalist order. Resources were largely allocated through the market, and most of them were privately owned. State intervention was ubiquitous, but it was designed to make capitalism work better, not to supersede it. Generous welfare states mitigated the rigors of market competition. The tamed capitalism that resulted would have been almost unrecognizable to the nineteenth-century paladins of laissez-faire, but it was capitalism all the same.

Thirdly, Western Europe was overwhelmingly democratic from the late 1940s onward, and universally so after the demise of Fascist regimes in Spain, Portugal, and Greece in the early 1980s. Lastly, the double victory of democracy and tamed capitalism was both child and parent of one of the most hopeful political projects of the twentieth century—the deliberate construction of a supranational European Community, based on law rather than force, in which ancient enemies could live together in peace.

That was the world in which today's policy makers and intellectuals grew up and whose contours they took for granted. It was a good world for the elites and peoples of the "West." Europe enjoyed a longer period of peace than at any time since the end of the Roman Empire. Throughout the "West," including its Asiatic honorary members, living standards were higher than they had ever been, and seemed set to rise indefinitely. Despite the cold war, a plethora of small hot wars, and a savage, medium-sized hot war in Vietnam, it was a remarkably stable world. Once the turbulent and unpredictable Soviet leader, Nikita Khrushchev, had left the scene, both superpowers tacitly agreed that, in the European cockpit, the frontier between the capitalist West and the Communist East should be inviolate. It was permissible to intervene in peripheral conflicts in the Third World. It was not permissible to try to change the balance of European power.

As a result, "western" policy makers and publics knew where they were. More important, they knew who they were. They did not always agree about their approach to the "East." Some wanted to confront it, others sought détente. But on fundamentals, they were at one. They knew that they belonged to the "West"; and that, as "westerners," they were free, democratic, progressive, tolerant, and prosperous. They thought they had learned how to retain the good in capitalism while jettisoning the bad. They saw themselves as children of the Enlightenment, champions of the Open Society. For them, the rhetoric of "West" and "East" was as natural as breathing. For obvious reasons, "eastern" elites did not use that rhetoric: it implied inferiority to the "West." But they too took it for granted that their world was different from that of the "West." And like their counterparts in the "West," they sought to manage the primordial conflict between the two, not to end it or transcend it—and still less to win it.

Then the earth shook. The great upheavals of 1989, which saw the fall of the Berlin Wall, and of 1991, when the Soviet Union imploded, destroyed the postwar world forever. For more than seventy years, Communism had been a practice as well as a doctrine. Communist ideology had challenged the democratic ideologies of the "West"; Communist practice had offered an alternative, working model of social organization—not just in an ideal world yet to be born, but in the quotidian reality of everyday life. It was not a particularly attractive alternative (at least not to "westerners"), but it did at least exist; and by existing it proved that the capitalist order was not the only possible one. The spectacular collapse of Communism throughout the huge territory once ruled by the Soviet Union and its satellites stood that proof on its head.

Suddenly, the alternative had disappeared—not because of foreign invasion or domestic revolt, but because its custodians had ceased to believe in it. The obvious conclusion was that it had always been a chimera—that the Marxist-Leninist God had been doomed to fail from the start. The Chinese story was less dramatic, but it had a similar dénouement. Under a nominally Communist party, the Chinese economy moved, ever more confidently, toward a strange kind of quasi-capitalism, run by a meritocratic but unaccountable and authoritarian elite. Capitalism was not just triumphant; for the first time since the Bolshevik Revolution, it was effectively unchallenged.

13

In Margaret Thatcher's Britain and Ronald Reagan's America, a restless, dynamic new version of the untamed capitalism of the nineteenth century had already started to edge aside the tamed capitalism of the postwar period. In the 1990s, capitalism's untaming forged ahead, on every continent and in virtually every country. From Murmansk to Mumbai and from New York to Novosibirsk, a new economic order was on the march. A new orthodoxy—that the rational pursuit of individual self-interest is the true source of economic efficiency, that the rising tide of wealth produced by undistorted markets lifts all boats, that markets should be set free to regulate themselves instead of being regulated by state authorities, and that government intervention in the economy does more harm than good—took the place of the orthodoxies of the postwar period. Growth burgeoned, inequality soared, and competition intensified, while capital vaulted over national frontiers. The universal victory of capitalism was mirrored in the global supremacy of the United States, the world's only remaining superpower. The cold war was over, it seemed, and the "West" had won.

Or had it? Militarily, the United States unquestionably towered over the rest of the world. It spent as much on defense as the next fifteen countries combined. American bases spanned the globe. The American economy was easily the biggest national economy in the world. It was more than three times as large as Japan's and more than four times that of Germany—though the total GDP of the "Eurozone," the fifteen-nation single-currency area at the heart of the European Union, ran it close. There was talk of a new American "empire," reminiscent of the British Empire of old days.[12] Some insisted that the global market, the heart and soul of the new capitalist order, needed a global hegemon to protect it and that the only conceivable hegemon was the United

States. The hidden hand of the market, as Thomas Friedman wrote, would not work without "a hidden fist."[13] A related argument was that only American power could protect the weak and punish the wicked: that, as Robert Kagan put it, the United States was the world's "sheriff." (Europe, he added, was its "saloon keeper.")[14] A simpler view was that, having become the world's only superpower, the United States was determined to stay that way: that America simply *was* a great power and was behaving as great powers always do.

At first hearing, the language seemed confident. Yet there was a distinct undertone of unease; and since the horror of 9/11, unease has been tinged increasingly with anxiety and at times with dread. Evidently, the end of the cold war had not procured immunity from danger after all. Despite her huge military arsenal, America was vulnerable; the city on a hill no longer enjoyed divine protection. Rogue states, failed states, and terrorist networks posed more alarming, because less predictable, threats to American security than had the cautious, almost comatose post-Khrushchev Soviet leadership. The Bush administration's answer was a new strategic doctrine, based on an explicit principle of "preemption," or preventive war. It was not enough to wait to be attacked and then fight back. It was necessary to take "anticipatory action"—if need be, "preemptively" and unilaterally.[15]

But despite the macho swaggering of its champions, the new doctrine was a sign of insecurity, not of confidence. The most spectacular example of "anticipatory action," namely the Iraq War, could hardly have been a worse advertisement for it. It appalled many American allies, dragged on far longer than its architects had expected, became increasingly unpopular with the American people, and, to cap it all, turned out to have been based on a mixture of deliberate deceit and faulty intelligence. When George W. Bush finally stepped down, the preemption doctrine and his own reputation were both in ruins. After his departure, revelations that CIA officers had routinely tortured Al Qaeda suspects left an even uglier stain on his—and America's—reputation. Meanwhile, Barack Obama, Bush's successor, made a breathtaking reversal of rhetoric and posture and abandoned macho swaggering in favor of modesty, flexibility, and inclusion. When he was awarded the Nobel Peace Prize in 2009, the world rejoiced. The era of the gun-toting global sheriff was over. America, it seemed, had rejoined the human race.

Obama was not just America's first black president. He was also the first global leader to belong, emotionally and existentially, to the diverse world of the twenty-first century—to a world whose most obvious features were the "rise of the rest" and a yawning gap between the old depiction of global power and a new reality.[16] While the new capitalism was rolling on, and "western" consumers and financiers were living high on the hog, a quiet revolution had begun to shift the balance of the global economy away from the "West" and toward the "East" and parts of the South. The so-called BRICS—Brazil, Russia, India, and China—were levering themselves up the global technological and economic ladder, much as the United States and Germany had done in the late nineteenth and early twentieth centuries.

Commentators did not all agree about the implications, but in late 2008 a remarkable report by the American National Intelligence Council summed up what had become a consensus view. It forecast that by 2025, the world's three largest economies would be the United States, China, and India, in that order. "In terms of size, speed, and directional flow," it declared, "the global shift in relative wealth and power—roughly from West to East—is without precedent in modern history." China and India "were restoring the positions they held two centuries ago. . . . The years around 2025 will be characterised by the dual identity of these Asian giants."[17] A peculiarly vivid example of what the new configuration of global power is likely to mean in practice came at the UN climate change conference in Copenhagen in December 2009, when the Chinese premier treated the United States—and, for that matter, many of the world's poorest and most exposed nations—with a mixture of lofty disdain and brutish contempt.

As the Intelligence Council's report was at pains to point out, the shift of power was relative, not absolute. In absolute terms, the United States is still—and is set to remain—very rich and very powerful. Relatively, however, it is in decline—economically most obviously, but politically as well. Obama's decency, intelligence, and grace have masked that decline, but they have not effaced the forces behind it. Not only did Obama fail to get his way at Copenhagen, but by the summer of 2010, more than a year into his presidency, he had also failed to break the logjam blocking peace between Israel and Palestine, one of his central objectives. And, as Britain discovered at the turn of the nineteenth and twentieth centuries, when Germany and the United States challenged her old economic supremacy, relative decline tends to be a painful and disorientating process. It is one thing to be the world's unchallenged top dog, another to watch newcomers to the kennels yapping at your heels.

The shattering global economic crisis that began in the summer of 2007, when the American investment bank Bear Stearns announced serious losses on its hedge funds and that felled the Wall Street giant Lehman Brothers in September 2008, has given the experience a harsher and more alarming edge. The lords of creation in the investment banks and hedge funds of Wall Street and the City of London were revealed, not just as greedy (that was hardly a surprise), but as credulous, mendacious, and sometimes fraudulent. The public authorities that were supposed to regulate them turned out to have been complacent and negligent. Above all, the economic theory that justified minimal regulation turned out to have been hopelessly flawed, as Alan Greenspan, chairman of the U.S. Federal Reserve from 1987 to 2006, admitted at a congressional hearing.[18]

Supposedly self-regulating markets had fostered a swelling orgy of risk taking that culminated in the near collapse of the world's financial system when the bubble burst. The seductive doctrine that the unhindered pursuit of individual self-interest holds the key to prosperity and growth had helped to procure the most devastating fall in output and employment for eighty years. The rational economic actor that economists put at the center of their conceptual universe had turned out to be a chimera. The financial services sector had been driven by the wild stampedes of what George Soros, the uncrowned king of hedge fund managers, called "the electronic herd."[19] J. M. Keynes's mordant warning against allowing capital investment to become "the by-product of a casino"[20] had turned out to be as pertinent in the 2000s as it had been in the 1930s. And, horror of horrors, it became clear that state intervention on a scale unprecedented in peacetime—including a plethora of bank nationalizations that would have been unthinkable before the crash—offered the only hope of rescuing the market economy from itself.

The roots of the crisis were deep, and the implications are still in debate. But one thing is clear. It was, above all, a crisis of the newly untamed capitalism, of the capitalism that had emerged in the 1980s and triumphed in the 1990s. It was not confined to the two pacemakers, the United States and Britain. Tiny Iceland was overwhelmed; mighty Germany was badly shaken. But when all the qualifications have been made, there is no doubt that the economic paradigm that collapsed so spectacularly was made in America: not for nothing was it known as the "Washington consensus." The heady mixture of greed, credulity, and self-destructive ingenuity that had loaded American banks with toxic assets and the American economy with a mountain of debt had plenty of European counterparts; the discovery that German banks had behaved as greedily and irresponsibly as their American and British counterparts made nonsense of the smug notion, much touted on the European mainland, that a special "Rhenish" capitalism was at one and the same time more kindly, less selfish, and more successful than the short-termist and hyper-individualistic Anglo-American model.[21]

But the fever was more flagrant in the United States (and still more so in Britain) than in mainland Europe. For years American and British commentators had berated Europe for failing to adopt the American model, while international institutions such as the IMF and the World Bank had lost no opportunity to pressure weaker nations to adopt it. Now its collapse had dragged the rest of the world down with it.

The full repercussions will not be known for some time. But it is already clear that the assumptions enshrined in Kipling's "Ballad of East and West" have been turned inside out. At the very heart of the West-East antimony of the last twenty-five hundred years lay the proposition that the "West" was par excellence the home of reason, efficiency, and evolutionary success: that an enlightened, modern, rational, and progressive "West" confronted an unenlightened and backward "East." These assumptions had always been patronizing and misleading. They are now manifestly absurd.

The financial crisis and all that flowed from it showed that—at least in the narrow terms of economic growth that the American model had itself privileged—"eastern" China and India were more efficient, more successful, and more rational than the supremely "western" United States. While Americans splurged, the Chinese had saved; indeed, without the flood of Chinese savings that poured into the United States, American splurging would have been impossible. And India had managed to combine economic success with a pulsating and rambunctious homegrown democracy, as vigorous as America's own.

The dynamism of the American economy, and the captivating resilience and openness of American society, had not suddenly disappeared, but the unique moral authority that America had enjoyed as the apparent epitome of rationality and progress, and which had underpinned her global hegemony, had suffered a terrible blow. As the Hong Kong property tycoon Ronnie Chan puts it, the world is in the throes of a subtle process of "rebalancing" moral authority. "The system that the west touted as superior," he writes, "has failed. Why should developing countries blindly follow its model now?"[22]

Political authority is "rebalancing" too. Madeleine Albright, Bill Clinton's secretary of state, once declared that the United States was "the indispensable nation." It is a safe bet that, for the foreseeable future, it will be *an* indispensable nation. But it will never again be alone in its eminence. "Eastern" China and India will be indispensable too: that was one of the lessons of the failure of the Copenhagen climate change conference. They may well be joined by "southern" Brazil and conceivably by "eastern" Russia as well. The obvious question for the United States as the pluralistic, unstable, conflicted world of the twenty-first century takes shape is Fareed Zakaria's. "Can Washington adjust and adapt to a world in which others have moved up? . . . Can it thrive in a world it cannot dominate?"[23] But there is also a less obvious and more painful question. Can Americans come to terms with the end of American exceptionalism? Can they abandon the myth of America as the city on a hill, with a unique, redemptive message for mankind? And can they do all this without damaging the patina of magic that still clings to their country?

The questions for America are hard enough, but the questions for Europe—the other half of the traditional "West"—are far harder. The familiar narrative of "West" and "East" had been European long before it crossed the Atlantic; the issues raised by the global transformation that is now making nonsense of it go to the heart of Europe's understanding of itself as well as of its place in the world. For the architects of the European project, Europe was not just part of the "West." It was the epitome of the "West": the heart and soul of the civilization that had first flowered in ancient Greece. Part of the point of the project was to enable Europe to recover its rightful place as the chief custodian of "western" values.

At the same time, "western" Europe could count on the support of a "western" superpower patron when the going got rough; the assumption that the patron will always be available to pull European chestnuts out of the fire is still part of the mind-set of Europe's leaders, particularly in the continent's eastern marches. But the emerging new global system has no place for such a patron. The Obama administration is not anti-European, as the neocons in the Bush administration used to be. However, it has new and bigger fish to fry.

21

The British commentator and historian Timothy Garton Ash puts it well: Obama, he writes, has "no sentimental attachment to the old continent. His question to Europe is: 'what can you do for us today?'"[24] And though Garton Ash does not say so, the answer is patently, "not much."

More probing questions follow. Can Europe recover the élan and political creativity that healed the wounds of the two great European civil wars of the last century and then extended the scope of democratic rule to the former Soviet satellites in East Central Europe? Can it overcome its internal contradictions—between European elites and their peoples, between democratic promise and technocratic reality? Can it develop institutions with the legitimacy, will, and capacity to enable it to join the United States, China, and India as a global power? Or is it doomed to remain an economic giant and a political pygmy—rich, fat, vulnerable, and increasingly irrelevant to the new world that is taking shape beyond its frontiers?

The current omens are not encouraging. The unique European experiment in consensual supranational government has been astonishingly successful. Old enemies *have* learned to live together, if not in fervent amity then at least in peace. Guaranteed human rights and the rule of law now prevail, albeit with occasional blemishes, right across the continent that spawned one of the most evil regimes in human history less than a lifetime ago. The trouble is that times have changed. The great, epochal successes of the European project took place, first in the binary world of the cold war and then in the monist world of unchallenged American primacy that followed: in other words, in an age when the old antimony of "West" versus "East" was virtually unchallenged. But that age is over. In today's conflicted and shifting world, the only dubiously legitimate governing institutions bequeathed by the Union's founding fathers—and still more the cluster of assumptions and habits that has grown up around them—are no longer fit for the vastly more daunting trials they face.

It took eight years—from 2001 to 2009—to devise and carry through a set of significant, but hardly earth-shattering, institutional reforms designed to make Union decision making more efficient and somewhat more transparent. The economic crisis of 2007–10 has shone a bright and cruel light on a design flaw in the Eurozone. As the Irish former EU commissioner Peter Sutherland caustically puts it, its system of governance is "intellectually and politically schizophrenic."[25] A European Central Bank controls monetary policy, but member governments still control fiscal policy. As a result, the weaker economies of the Eurozone are caught in a vice. They cannot let their currencies float downward in response to the global crisis, as Britain did: they have no currencies of their own. But there is no supranational budget to help them mitigate the deflationary consequences of the crisis as there are in fully fledged federations. And, to cap it all, Europe was sidelined at the Copenhagen climate change conference. Though European politicians frequently talk about the shift of economic and political power from west to east, there is little sign that they or the citizens they represent have thought seriously about its implications for European political economies or the Union's curious constitution. In Brussels and the capitals of the member states, the dominant theme is "business as usual," or at least "business as usual, as soon as we can get back to it."

Sober reflection on the implications of the changing configuration of global power has been drowned out by a chorus of self-congratulation. Many hold that the European Union's undoubted success in persuading national lambs to lie down with once-threatening national lions can and should be indefinitely repeated in the territories beyond its present frontiers, and that its vocation is to carry the message of that success to the rest of humanity. The distinguished German sociologist, Ulrich Beck, has opined that "the catch-phrase for the future might be 'Move Over America—Europe is back'"; the brilliant young British publicist, Mark Leonard, has insisted that "a New European Century" is dawning and that Europe "will run the 21st century"; while the Frenchman, Marcel Gauchet, editor of *Le Débat*, has prophesied that the formula pioneered in Europe will eventually serve as "a model for the nations of the world. That lies in its genetic programme."[26] But, to cooler heads, this enlightened, postnational vocation looks as Eurocentric as the unenlightened, imperialistic vocation that dazzled Europeans in the nineteenth century. It also seems remarkably reminiscent of the American dream of the city on a hill and, if anything, even less likely to play well with the rising powers of Asia and Latin America. The kindest thing to say about such dreams of Europe as a light to lighten the gentiles in the rest of the world is that they are a century out-of-date.

On present trends, the American National Intelligence Council thought, Europe will be "losing clout in 2025," while the EU will likely remain a "hobbled giant, distracted by internal bickering and competing national agendas."[27] To be sure, these trends are not set in stone. Few in the devastated Europe of 1946 or 1947 would have predicted the astonishing upsurge in living standards that transformed the western half of the continent in the 1950s and 1960s. In the querulous 1970s, few foresaw that, by the end of the century, a single European currency would replace national currencies throughout the continent's heartland—a tragically incomplete achievement as I suggested a moment ago, but nevertheless a historic one. As late as the summer of 1989, no one imagined that the then Communist states of East Central Europe would soon become full members of the Union, pledged to democracy and the rule of law. Trends can bend. Europe's fate is in its own hands. But it can prove the doomsters wrong only by drawing on all its reserves of political creativity and imagination.

Imagination matters most. The architects of the European project were hardheaded politicians and officials, not otherworldly dreamers. But they were politicians and officials with a difference. They had an exceptional capacity to see beyond their noses: to imagine a different future and a path toward it. Events did not follow their path in every respect: it would have been astonishing if they had. Yet the two great changes of the recent past—enlargement to the east and the single currency—were immanent in their project from the beginning. The Europe of 2011 is the product of the leap of imagination that brought the European Community into existence nearly sixty years ago.

But sixty years is a long time. Another leap is long overdue. The great question is what form it should take. This book offers one man's answer. I examine the contradictions and evasions in which the European Union is now enmeshed and suggest an alternative approach. But my alternative is open-ended. I do not set out a ready-made blueprint for the future, still less a toolbox of institutional quick fixes. My focus is on the ideas, memories, and *assumptions* that shape the thinking of policy makers and institution leaders rather than on policies or institutions themselves. And I write as a committed friend of the European project, not as a foe. The last thing I want to do is to denigrate its achievements or to belittle the moral vision that lies at its heart. But I believe that the best way to pursue that vision as this troubled century moves on is to sound the alarm. Self-congratulation is no longer enough.

# -II-

## WEIGHING LIKE A NIGHTMARE

Men make their own history, but they do not make it just as they please,
they do not make it under circumstances chosen by themselves.... The
tradition of all the dead generations weighs like a nightmare on the brain
of the living.

—Karl Marx, *The Eighteenth Brumaire of Louis Bonaparte*, 1852

On March 26, 2007, Europe's leaders assembled in Berlin to
celebrate the fiftieth anniversary of the Rome Treaty setting
up the European Economic Community, the precursor of today's European Union. They did their best to avoid triumph-
alism, but the mood was upbeat. In a resounding anniversary
declaration, the assembled leaders insisted that for centuries,
Europe had been "an idea, holding out hope of peace and
understanding." That hope, they added, "has been fulfilled."
Following the meeting, José Manuel Barroso, the president of
the Brussels-based European Commission, declared that the
EU had procured "peace, liberty and prosperity beyond the
dreams of even the most optimistic founding fathers."[1]

Empty boasting? Or sober fact? The inconvenient truth
is that it was both. The story is long and convoluted—much
longer and more convoluted than the assembled leaders
may have realized or than the average EU citizen could have
imagined. It is a story of exemplary political courage and

remarkable successes. It is also one of institutional paralysis and well-merited failure. It goes back to the horrors of the two world wars, to the clashing ethnic and national ambitions of the late nineteenth and early twentieth centuries, and even to the bloody exploits of Napoleon and Louis XIV. To help tease out its enduring significance, I shall frame it with mental journeys to two of the most evocative sites of memory (*lieux de mémoire*) on the European continent.

The first is to the former garrison town of Verdun in northeastern France. In 1916, French forces at Verdun halted and eventually turned back a German onslaught in the most terrible battle ever fought on the European continent west of the old Soviet Union. According to Alistair Horne's classic *The Price of Glory*, Verdun was the longest battle in human history—twice as long as Stalingrad. The combined casualties of the French and Germans together reached the staggering total of more than 700,000. Killed or missing totaled more than 260,000. A plaque on one of the forts that circled the town, placed there by an unknown French mother, but since removed, said everything that needed to be said: "To my son, since your eyes were closed mine have never ceased to cry."[2]

In the huge and forbidding Ossuary on the site of the battle lie the remains of 150,000 unidentified dead. But the single most moving artifact in the Ossuary building is an iconic picture of Helmut Kohl (then German chancellor) and François Mitterrand (then president of France) holding hands, each carrying an immense wreath in his other hand and each facing the camera with an expression of profound grief. They were, of course, mourning the dead of both their countries and paying tribute to the astonishing courage of the troops engaged in the battle. But they were also doing something else. They were celebrating the greatest single achievement of the postwar European project—the reconciliation between France and Germany, whose rivalry had lain at the heart of the European civil war that devastated the continent twice in the space of less than thirty years and had been a central theme of European history since the days of Louis XIV. For Verdun was not alone. Again and again, the fields of Flanders and northeastern France have been drenched in blood: Malplaquet, Sedan, Ypres, the Somme, and the Marne all tell the same story of doomed young men slaughtered in a seemingly primordial struggle for supremacy between Frenchmen and Germans. In East Central Europe, Jena, Austerlitz, and Leipzig tell it too.

The road to reconciliation was circuitous and stony. In the immediate aftermath of World War II, Germany was prostrate and France battered and impoverished. The last thing French elites wanted was to be reconciled with Germany. German armies had swept through northeastern France and threatened Paris three times in the space of a human lifetime. Twice, France had been defeated and occupied. Once she had beaten off the hereditary enemy, but only at an enormous cost in French lives. French elites and people were determined that the same thing should not happen a fourth time. They wanted to keep Germany in subjection and to modernize French industry at her expense. It was only when the United States insisted that West Germany's recovery was fundamental to the Western cause in the cold war that France changed her tune.

But the change, when it came, was total and dramatic. In one of the boldest strokes in postwar European history, France hit on a new solution to her perennial German problem. It was the brainchild of the head of the French Planning Commission, the rotund, dapper former cognac salesman, financier, and international troubleshooter, Jean Monnet.

Germany and France would *both* hand over control of their coal and steel industries—in those days the sinews of national power—to a supranational High Authority, in charge of a European Coal and Steel Community, whose embrace would also cover the Low Countries and Italy. France would be saved from the threat of a resurgent and hostile Germany. Germany would be saved from herself. From that acorn grew the tender sapling of the European Economic Community and then the jagged oak of today's European Union.

Monnet's scheme did not descend from a totally clear sky. In the 1790s, the austere Prussian philosopher Immanuel Kant had argued that a steadily expanding federation of republican states could secure perpetual peace. Before the First World War, the German Social Democrat Karl Kautsky called for a United States of Europe, complete with a federal parliament and an army. In the 1920s, the Austrian count Coudenhove-Kalergi launched a Pan-European Movement. In 1930, the then French foreign minister, Aristide Briand, had put forward a plan to unite Europe. In western Europe, at least, the Nazi New Order during World War II can be seen as a brutish proto–common market.

Meanwhile, anti-Nazi resistance movements were drawn to federalism as the only way to end the bitter cycle of war, resentment, and revenge of which Hitler's aggression was the latest manifestation. The Italian Resistance adopted a manifesto advocating a European federation once the war was over.[3] Similar ideas circulated in the German Kreisau Circle, many of whose members took part in the famous July Plot to assassinate Hitler in 1944 and were tortured and butchered by the Gestapo when the plot failed. But none of this detracts from Monnet's achievement, or from that of Robert Schuman, the shy, devoutly Catholic French foreign minister to whom Monnet sold his brainchild. Between them, as François Duchêne has put it, these two "switched the points of European state-craft traditional since the late Middle Ages."[4]

It is hard to exaggerate the significance of the Franco-German reconciliation for "Europe," as idea and as fact. It lay at the heart of the European project; its achievement did more than any other single thing to produce the longest period of peace and prosperity in post-Roman European history—at least in the western half of the continent. And the *method* was as remarkable as the achievement itself. The founding fathers of the EU did not seek to abolish national sovereignty in the way that the founding fathers of the United States had abolished the sovereignty of the constituent states. They wished to transcend it—an astounding political innovation whose inner meaning has been so swathed in rebarbative academic jargon and even more rebarbative officialese that only a tiny minority of the Union's citizens understand how it works.

Yet the essentials are clear. The first and primary aim of the whole exercise, as Monnet put it himself, was to bring "France and Germany together and exorc[ise] the demons of the past."[5] The exorcists would bring the ancient rivals together within a new, nonimperial version of the early medieval empire of Charlemagne, united by consent instead of force and governed through a grindingly complex process of negotiation and power-sharing between still-sovereign states and supranational institutions. France would be protected from the threat of German revanchism; Germany would receive a desperately needed certificate of international respectability. The empire would be led by France, but only by virtue of the astonishing brilliance and creativity of the elites that ran the French state—and of the mixture of modesty and guilt that suffused the elites of the weak, new, postwar German state.

31

The project worked. The Coal and Steel Community was set up in 1952. The failure of a French plan to set up a European Defence Community in 1954 was canceled out by the creation of the European Economic Community in 1957. Autarchic tariff barriers restricting trade between the six founding member states came down more quickly than anyone expected. A common agricultural policy and external tariff were soon in place. But these successes have often been misunderstood. The member states of the new Community—and, above all, the two prime movers—did not lose power to a ghostly, supranational entity called "Brussels," as many on both sides of the argument imagined. On the contrary, they gained it. As the British economic historian, Alan Milward, has argued, state capacities in Community Europe grew dramatically in the decade and a half after the establishment of the Coal and Steel Community. Gone were the fragile, penurious, and barely legitimate states of the early postwar period. Their successors—the stable, thriving European states of the 1960s, with their increasingly interdependent economies and rising prosperity—were more able to achieve their purposes and more firmly rooted in popular support than any European states before them.[6] But they had gained power by sharing it.

Integration faltered in the 1970s, but in the 1980s and 1990s, it speeded up. A European Monetary System (EMS) was set up in 1978 to create a zone of currency stability in Europe. The Single European Act of 1986 abolished national vetoes over a wide range of policy fields. A renewed push toward a genuinely single market, involving the free movement of goods, capital, and labor throughout the Community territory, followed in its wake. In 1992, the Maastricht Treaty set the seal on these achievements—symbolically by transforming the

"Community" into a "Union" and practically by setting out a path to full monetary union. The year 1999 saw the launch of the euro. In 2002, euro notes and coins replaced national ones. By 2007, on the eve of the financial and economic crisis that engulfed the world after the collapse of Lehman Brothers, more than 26 percent of the world's official foreign exchange reserves were held in euros. The Eurozone's total GDP was second only to that of the United States.

There was more. Shortly after Britain joined the then European Community, a senior British judge compared Community membership to "an incoming tide. It flows into the estuaries and up the rivers. It cannot be held back."[7] It was a telling metaphor. The European project has exerted massive, if often hidden, influence on the political cultures and assumptions of the member states. To take just one striking example, the popular referendum has become part of the famously unwritten constitution of the United Kingdom—undermining the old tradition of absolute parliamentary sovereignty—largely because deep divisions over membership of the European Community could not be settled by conventional parliamentary means. The effect on Germany was much more striking. Old notions of historically determined German exceptionalism—of a German *Sonderweg* or special path, embodying uniquely German and essentially undemocratic values—have perished.

Perhaps this would have happened in any case. Germany's crushing defeat and unconditional surrender undoubtedly helped to convince Germans that the *Sonderweg* of old days had led to disaster. But defeat and occupation could not, in themselves, offer a positive alternative to dreams of German exceptionalism. Peaceful integration into a partially supranational Europe, committed to pluralist democracy and the rule of law, could and did. For many Germans, Europeanism became a surrogate patriotism. In a famous phrase, the great German novelist Thomas Mann declared, "Our aim is not a German Europe, but a European Germany." That became a theme song for a generation of Germans.

Britain and Germany are not alone. Everywhere, policy making on the national level now intersects with policy making on the Union level. On every weekday, national ministers and civil servants can be found in overheated rooms, in ugly office blocks in Brussels, negotiating with their opposite numbers from other member states, and with officials from the European Commission and Council. A myriad other national institutions—NGOs, trade unions, business firms, farmers' organizations, local authorities, environmental campaigners, and the like—also take part in the endless process of bargaining and coalition building that shapes Union policy. An endless flood of EU decisions cascades from Brussels to the parliaments of the member states, which then transmute them into national law. According to one estimate, almost 80 percent of Irish national legislation originated in EU decisions in 2008.[8] In Britain, around half of UK legislation affecting business, charities, and the voluntary sector stems from decisions taken by Union bodies—which, of course, include British members of the European Parliament and ministers.[9] The wheeler-dealing takes place within a framework of European law, interpreted by a European Court of Justice (ECJ), which has deliberately modeled itself on the U.S. Supreme Court. European law takes precedence over national laws; ECJ decisions bind national courts and national governments. As well, national courts themselves apply EU law and act, in effect, as ECJ agents. Individual citizens can and do bring cases to the ECJ, and its judgments can force member governments to change unjust policies *within* their own territories.

A good example of what this means in practice came in 1995 when the European Court found in favor of a British citizen who had alleged that the British government had acted improperly in denying free prescriptions to men until the age of sixty-five, when women received them at age sixty. Since then, men have been treated in the same way as women. A comparatively small matter in itself, perhaps, but another portentous breach in the dike of national sovereignty. The EU is not a federal state, but as this episode shows, it is far more than a loose-knit confederation of the sort that preceded the creation of the United States, in which the central power was little more than a club of state ambassadors. Indeed, it is almost certainly more integrated than was the United States itself at an equivalent stage in American history. (To take only one obvious example, there are no slave states in the EU.)

The most remarkable testimony to the generative powers of the Monnet-Schuman acorn is the Union's extraordinary capacity to attract new members. However tame and tedious it may look from inside, it has been a beacon of promise to outsiders. A long line of countries on its periphery has applied successfully for membership, not because anyone forced them to but because they thought they would be better off inside. The founding fathers' Europe of the Six (France, Germany, Italy, Holland, Belgium, and Luxembourg) became nine in 1973, with the accession of Britain, Denmark, and Ireland. By the early eighties, Greece, Spain, and Portugal had brought the total to twelve. Now the EU has twenty-seven member states. Its frontiers extend from the Blasket Islands off the west coast of Ireland to the Belarussian border, and from the Arctic Circle to Cyprus. Throughout its territory, even in former Communist satellites with weak or nonexistent democratic traditions, democracy and the rule of law prevail (albeit smirched, in some cases, by endemic corruption and resentful populism).

The Union's population totals around 500 million, and its combined GDP more than $16 trillion—about $2 trillion more than that of the United States. It is easily the largest trading bloc in the world. The continent is more united now than it was in Roman days; a humdrum process of peaceful negotiation and compromise has done what all Napoleon's armies failed to do. I worked in the European Commission for a short time in the 1970s. If I had forecast that the next thirty years would see progress on the scale the Union has experienced, I would have been thought insane.

My second mental journey, this time to Auschwitz and Auschwitz-Birkenau in southern Poland, comes into the story at this point. It is a grim and horrifying place. The piles of human hair, artificial limbs, and shoes leave an indelible impression. But for me, the sheer, vast expanse of Auschwitz-Birkenau—around 340 acres—was more horrifying than anything else. Auschwitz is, of course, a symbol of the Holocaust, about which there is a mountain of scholarly literature and over which there are searching debates. (It is not the only symbol: a total of around 1.5 million Jews were killed in the death camps of Treblinka, Belzec, and Sobibor, a larger number than in Auschwitz.)[10] I shall not contribute to the mountain or take part in the debates. What matters, for my purposes, is that Auschwitz and the other Nazi death camps were there, that the Holocaust took place, and that it was a central reality of European history in the twentieth century. Nearly six million Europeans were deliberately and systematically killed, in a process of industrialized mass murder, in the name of ethnic and racial purity, and of the belief that a pitiless, never-ending struggle for supremacy between rival races was the motor of history. There have been plenty of other evils in European history—the crusade against the Albigensians, the wars of religion of the sixteenth and seventeenth centuries, and the slave trade, to mention only a few. But none of them equaled the Holocaust in horror.

However, the nature of the horror is often misunderstood. The "anti-Semitism" that led to the Holocaust was quite different from the age-old Judaeophobia that went back to the Middle Ages and even the late Roman Empire. Medieval Judaeophobia was a special case of xenophobia—of fear of and hatred for "others." In an age when it was taken for granted that morality, the social order, religious belief, and the divinely created cosmos itself were intertwined—and when the teachings and rites of the Church were part of the texture of life—the presence of patent non-Christians in the midst of Christian societies was peculiarly unsettling and sometimes threatening. (Christian heresies were equally threatening for the Church, and Christian heretics were treated at least as cruelly as were Jews, and often more so.)

Religion was not a private matter, for Jews or for Christians. Jewish Law presupposed a Jewish community, however small. The Christian revelation was given tangible, dramatic form in the weekly miracle of the Eucharist as well as in a myriad public festivals that offered dignity and meaning to the meanest as well as to the mighty. The two faiths were "siblings,"[11] but they were also rivals. Each challenged the very essence of the other. If Christianity were true, then Judaism was false: Christ had appeared among the Jews, and the Jews had rejected him. If Judaism were true, Christianity was false: Christ was an imposter and his teachings a travesty of divine law. However, dreams of ethnic purity had no place in this mental universe. Jews might be confined to ghettoes, forcibly converted, occasionally even burned at the stake. But no one thought they belonged to an inferior *race*, doomed by their genes.

The notion of an ethnically pure nation-state would have been incomprehensible to medieval Judaeophobes. There were no nation-states—indeed no states at all in the modern sense of the term—before the sixteenth century; and no one dreamed, or could have dreamed, of ethnic purity as a basis of statehood. (The obsession with "purity of the blood" in early-modern, ferociously Catholic Spain was an ugly but peculiarly Iberian foretaste of twentieth-century horrors.) Medieval Europe was a patchwork quilt of overlapping jurisdictions—the Church, the Empire, a variety of more or less powerful Crowns, principalities, cities, bishoprics, and so on, all jumbled up. It was, by definition, multiethnic and also multicultural. Jews were part of the jumble. They suffered continuous harassment and bouts of brutal persecution; they were tolerated at one moment, only to be expelled at another. At times of religious exaltation, as at the launch of the First Crusade, they could become targets of murderous popular rage. Sometimes they were welcomed, as by the rulers of ostentatiously Christian Poland.

"Anti-Semitism" is different. It is the ugly, irredeemably evil face of the nineteenth-century liberal belief that ethnically defined "nations" had a right to self-determination—a belief that seemed self-evident and fundamental to Woodrow Wilson, and that helped to shape the doom-laden Versailles settlement.[12] Modern anti-Semitism often drew on old Judaeophobic stereotypes, but it was not, in itself, a reversion to medieval primitivism. The people it mobilized were not all lumpen thugs or twisted sadists. Among them were highly educated, highly civilized scientists, doctors, lawyers, and philosophers, by no means all of them German. For these, the Nazis were the future, while the decadent democracies of the West were mired in the past. Nazism spelled classless solidarity, national renewal, steel and concrete, virile young men marching in harmony, cars speeding along Hitler's motorways, and Leni Riefenstahl's spectacular and chilling propaganda film, *Triumph of the Will*. By the same token, Nazi anti-Semitism seemed "modern" and "scientific," grounded in the inescapable realities of biology. It was the dark side of a widely held conception of modernity, scientific truth, and popular government—the product of a witches' brew of perverted Darwinism and perverted tribal democracy.

And particularly of the latter. The democratic promise of self-government has always had an ambiguity at its heart: who are the demos? Individuals living in a defined slice of territory? Or an ethnically defined group, which might well cut across territorial boundaries? Democrats in France and the United Kingdom gave the first answer. In the multiethnic empires of the Romanovs, the Hapsburgs, the Ottomans, and the Hohenzollerns, most of them were bound to give the second. Theirs was the democracy of the *Volk*, the tribe, the *ethnos*. Inevitably so: ethnic boundaries cut across imperial ones; emotionally and morally, popular government and national liberation seemed different sides of the same coin. Poles sought self-government for Poles and Rumanians for Rumanians, irrespective of the empire they happened to inhabit and whose yoke they yearned to throw off.[13] In a more complicated way, much the same was true of Germans. German nationalism was born in the wars of liberation against Napoleon; as such it was inherently exclusive. Central to it was "the need to ensure the internal cohesion of the tribe" and to "put a high premium on rigorously defining the outsider."[14]

In these struggles, the Jews had no place. Once the discourse of tribal democracy, ethnic nationalism, and ethnic self-determination took hold, as it did spectacularly in the closing months of World War I and at the peace conference that followed, the Jews were anomalous, strangers at the feast. They were marginal at best and potentially dangerous at worst. They were too numerous to be ignored and not numerous (or geographically concentrated) enough to sustain a claim to an ethnic state of their own. Self-styled "Zionists" sought an ethnically Jewish state in Palestine on the model of the ethnically Slavic states of East Central Europe. The Zionist project received a powerful boost when, with shameless duplicity, the British government declared that it favored the establishment of a "national home for the Jewish people" in Palestine, having previously promised that it would be part of an Arab kingdom. (It is hardly necessary to add that the indigenous population was not consulted.)

But this did not make the Jewish presence in the raw, ethnically nationalist states of East Central Europe any less anomalous; if anything it made it more so. The anomaly was not *bound* to lead to the peculiarly evil version of anti-Semitism espoused by the Nazis, but the connection was close. The Holocaust was the ultimate horror to which the notion of ethnic purity and of the nation-state as the embodiment of ethnic purity had led.

It was by no means the only one, however. In Nazi eyes, Slavs as well as Jews were *Untermenschen*, destined for slavery if not always for murder. Soviet prisoners of war perished in Auschwitz too; indeed, they supplied the first victims of the Zyklon B gas later used to murder Jews. Of the 5.2 million Soviet prisoners of war captured by the Germans, at least 2 million died in captivity, many of them shot in cold blood. Poles fared at least as badly. For Hitler, the Poles were "[m]ore animals than human beings. . . . The filth of Poles is unimaginable."[15] Educated Poles were systematically singled out for killing; altogether around 10 percent of the ethnic Polish population perished. The death toll among Gypsies was even higher: altogether, the Nazis murdered around a quarter of Europe's Gypsy population.[16] The barbarities meted out to the non-Jewish populations of occupied western Europe did not plumb the depths reached in eastern Europe, but as the tide of battle turned against Germany, savage SS reprisals for attacks by the French Resistance mirrored similar reprisals farther east. The most notorious occurred in June 1944, in the Limousin commune of Oradour-sur-Glane, where the SS massacred all the inhabitants they could find, including women and children, then set their bodies alight and torched the town.

The murderous potential of ethnic nationalism was realized most fully in Nazi Germany, but there were plenty of other examples. Stalin's Soviet Union was not a professedly ethnically nationalist state like Nazi Germany; on the contrary, it claimed to incarnate a supra-ethnic ideology promising liberation to the proletariat of all lands. Even so, there was a strong ethnic bias in the regime's mass killings: significantly higher proportions of Poles, Belarussians, and Ukrainians were killed than of ethnic Russians.[17] And German prisoners of war in the Soviet Union fared almost as badly as Russian prisoners in Germany: out of the 3.2 million German prisoners, 1.2 million died in captivity. Around 110,000 German women were raped by Soviet soldiers in the flush of victory after Berlin had fallen to them.[18] The Croat fascist Ustashe murdered 200,000 Serbs and large numbers of Muslims. After the war, Germans were forced out of their homes in the Sudetenland, Silesia, Transylvania, Yugoslavia, Romania, and parts of Prussia. Altogether, more than 11 million Germans were expelled from eastern and central Europe, often with extreme brutality; between 500,000 and 1,000,000 of them perished.[19] The British had never yearned for an ethnically pure state for themselves, but they were not immune to the ethnic hatreds that swirled across the European mainland in the war years. Their "carpet" or "area" bombing of German cities was deliberately designed to kill as many civilians as possible; to that end, the RAF Bomber Command dropped 955,000 tons of bombs altogether.

Grisly parodies of Nazism marked the German puppet-state of Vichy France. It abandoned the republican motto of *liberté, egalité, fraternité* in favor of *travail, famille, patrie* and collaborated with shameful enthusiasm in the Holocaust. A similar parody was enacted in Norway, where another German puppet, Vidkun Quisling, emulated Nazi anti-Semitism and anti-Marxism. The true message of Auschwitz for present-day Europe is not just that nearly six million Jews were murdered in the Holocaust. It is that ethnic nationalism can brutalize and kill.

The European project was not a direct response to the Holocaust. When it started, the Holocaust was the elephant in the European room from which everyone—even the victims—averted their eyes. The survivors did not wish to talk about it. Nor did the Israelis; and nor did non-Jewish Europeans. But their reticence was only one facet of a more complex truth. The language of *realpolitik* and *raison d'état* that I used to describe the statecraft of Schuman, Konrad Adenauer, and Alcide de Gasperi cannot capture the full meaning of the drive toward European union in the postwar years. That language is indispensable, but it must not be allowed to drown out less precise and more emotionally charged languages: realpolitik is never practiced in a cultural and moral vacuum. To understand the transformation of Europe between 1950 and 1970, we must think ourselves back into the intellectual and moral context in which it began and imagine what it was like to emerge, battered and exhausted, from the wartime barbarities of which the Holocaust was the most extreme example.

Europeans had supped on horrors. No one had to tell them that unbridled ethnic nationalism was largely to blame. They knew. The promoters of the European project knew it too. They sought to transcend, not just the sovereign nation-state but ethnic nationalism as such: to enable different ethnicities to live side by side in peace in a borderless space, in which people, goods, services, and capital could move freely. In time, they hoped, national barriers to free movement would go the way of the ancient local and provincial barriers that had disappeared during the course of nineteenth-century nation building.

The vision that inspired Jean Monnet—the most important of the Union's founding fathers—was summed up in the motto he chose for his memoirs: "Nous ne coalisons pas des Etats, nous unissons les hommes" (We are not building a coalition of States; we are uniting men). Echoing his vision, the Rome Treaty declared that the purpose of the exercise was to lay the foundations for an "ever close union" of the peoples of Europe. In this union, the French would still be French, the Germans German, and the Italians Italian, but they would also share a common *European* identity, reflecting common European values, a common European civilization, and a common commitment to the European project. Little by little, the shared, supranational European identity would come to trump the separate national identities embodied in the constituent states, just as national identities had, over time, trumped premodern provincial or local identities. For Europe was more than a geographical expression. It was also an idea—and an ideal.

Monnet's vision has fared better than his readers could have expected when his memoirs were published more than thirty years ago. French football stars play for British teams. The *Financial Times* is a continental as well as a British paper. The death penalty has been outlawed throughout the European Union. Albeit with national variations, a distinct European social model, profoundly different from the harsher American approach to social welfare, is deeply rooted throughout the continent, though less so in the former Communist countries of East Central Europe than in the European heartland. The free movement of goods, capital, and labor is part of the texture of European life. Polish lorries thunder down the French A6 on their way to Spain; Slovenian lorries pass through the Channel Tunnel on their way to the North of England. About 1.2 million students have taken part in the EU's Erasmus program for student exchanges. The Bologna Process, designed to make European university courses and accreditation qualifications interchangeable, covers the entire EU as well as a number of other European states—even including Russia. EU citizens are entitled to vote in European and local elections in member states other than their own. They are also entitled to publicly funded health care throughout the Union's territory.

The early 2000s saw a huge influx of Polish workers into Britain and a slightly smaller influx of French ones. Around 600,000 Britons own houses in Spain and a similar number in France. (It is not for nothing that the area around Calais is sometimes known as "south Kent.") Under the Schengen Agreement, border controls between all but five member states of the Union have been abolished. Fifteen of these twenty-two countries, together with Cyprus, also belong to the Eurozone. Despite the shocks inflicted on the euro in late 2009 and early 2010, you can travel from Barcelona to Berlin using the same currency wherever you go, and from Rome to Riga without producing a passport. Europe has not become an American-style melting pot. As anyone traveling on a French high-speed train, drinking in an Irish pub, or eating Polish bigos will soon discover, its ancient diversity, reflected in the varied blends of innovation and tradition that give European life its special flavor, still survives. Yet in mainland Europe, national boundaries are more porous today than they have ever been, expanding minds, widening opportunities, and enriching cultures.

But there is a worm in the bud. Everywhere there are signs of a potentially fatal *disconnect* dividing the peoples of Europe from the European elites. One obvious example is the turnout in elections to the European Parliament (a nominated body until 1979 but directly elected since). Turnout has been declining steadily since the first EP elections in 1979—from almost 65 percent in 1979 to just under 50 percent in 1999 and to 43 percent in the most recent EP elections in 2009. And turnout has been particularly low in the new member states in East Central Europe. (It was less than 20 percent in Slovakia.) Yet in the thirty years since the first elections to the European Parliament, its role and powers have grown out of all recognition. Almost all Union legislation is now subject to "co-decision" between the Parliament and the Council of Ministers—meaning that the Parliament's legislative powers are now equal to those of the member governments. By an extraordinary paradox, in short, dwindling turnout has gone hand in hand with growing power.

A more ominous example is the fate of the so-called Constitutional Treaty, designed to streamline the Union's arcane decision-making processes, to strengthen protections for human rights, and to raise Europe's global profile by creating a new post of EU foreign minister. The Treaty was backed by all the member governments and most of the Union's political leaders, but in the summer of 2005 it was rejected in referendums, first by a substantial majority in France and then by a crushing one in the Netherlands. The French result was a particularly cruel blow. Apart from a hiatus during de Gaulle's presidency, France had been at the forefront of the integration process since it began. Without her, there would have been no Coal and Steel Community, no Economic Community, and almost certainly no Monetary Union. Now, it seemed, the French people had spurned their own leaders' greatest achievement.

In 2007 the EU governments negotiated a "European Reform Treaty" (commonly known as the Lisbon Treaty), not very different in essentials from the Constitutional Treaty that the French and Dutch electorates rejected. But the new Treaty was carefully designed to present as narrow a front as possible to Euro-skeptic opposition, and it was clear that the governments were desperately anxious to avoid a searching debate on its implications. Their reward was as cruel as it was unexpected. Only Ireland held a referendum on the Lisbon Treaty; and to the shocked amazement of the Irish political class, almost all of which had urged a yes vote, the Irish voted against the Treaty by 53 percent to 47 percent. Calculation of the costs and benefits of EU membership played little part in the result. A flowing tide of EU funds had poured into Ireland since her accession in 1973, helping to transform it from a poverty-stricken backwater into an apparently lusty "Celtic tiger." (Appearances turned out to be deceptive: by October 2008, Ireland was in deep recession. But the tiger's approaching sickness was not an issue in the referendum campaign.)

EU membership had also enabled Ireland to escape from the resented shadow of its British neighbor and to play an independent and sometimes distinguished role in European politics. But such arguments had cut no ice in the referendum campaign. The Irish had voted with their hearts, not with their heads; and their hearts had told them that it was time to humble their overwhelmingly Europhile elite and rein in the Union structures in which it was enmeshed. In 2009, after Europe's leaders had given a chastened Dublin government binding guarantees so as to meet Irish concerns over abortion, neutrality, and the size of the European Commission,[20] a large majority of Irish voters voted yes in another referendum, and the Treaty was duly ratified. But it was hard to believe that Irish hearts had softened. Almost certainly, their heads had told them that it was wise to cling to their European nurse during the worst economic blizzard for eighty years.

Disconnect has gone hand in hand with division. To be sure, the member governments have never been wholly at one. In the early days of the Community, France's magnificently obdurate President de Gaulle was frequently a spoke in the wheel of the European carriage. He kept Britain out of the Community against the wishes of the other member governments, frustrated their attempt to institute majority voting in its Council of Ministers, and withdrew France from NATO'S integrated military command (though not from NATO itself). In the 1980s, Britain's prime minister, Margaret Thatcher, became a rather less magnificent but equally obdurate de Gaulle in skirts, hammering the European Commission for its alleged corporatism, and its president, Jacques Delors, for his openly federalist ambitions. But on the great issues of geopolitics, differences between the member states were symbolic, not substantive: everyone (even de Gaulle) knew that the entire western half of the Continent sheltered behind the United States, and no one offered a serious challenge to the transatlantic alliance or to the postwar global order.

The fall of Communism liberated Europeans from dependence on American power. But hopes that they would discover an independent geopolitical vocation of their own were soon disappointed. In the savage, occasionally genocidal Balkan wars that accompanied the breakup of the former Yugoslavia—wars that took place on the EU's doorstep—the Union succumbed to an ignominious paralysis as member states bickered among themselves. In the end, American intervention saved the day, both over Bosnia and over Kosovo, but that only underlined the EU's ignominy.

Then came the greater humiliation of the 2003 Iraq War. The EU member states did not just bicker; their divisions split the Union in two. Of the four big member states, the British and Italian governments fell into line behind the United States—Britain's with an extraordinary mixture of willful subservience and messianic zeal. The governments of France and Germany were passionately against the war. The Netherlands were in favor, Belgium against; Greece and Austria were against, Spain and Portugal in favor. The candidate members in the former Communist bloc—famously dubbed "New Europe" by the flat-footed, neoconservative American defense secretary, Donald Rumsfeld—also joined President Bush's "coalition of the willing." Tempers in both camps cooled as time went on. But there was no denying that the dream of a common Union foreign policy had failed its first really serious test.

It is too soon to tell how the worldwide economic crisis will impinge on Europe. But two things are clear. The first is that the market fundamentalism of the last thirty years has been discredited. Everywhere, the cry has gone up for government action to avert the threat of a 1930s-style depression. Unfortunately, the second point of clarity is that, thanks to the design flaw in the Eurozone that I mentioned in the previous chapter, the governments of the weaker EU economies are trapped in the straitjacket of an overvalued currency that inhibits the Keynesian pump priming that the times demand, and may force them into economically disastrous and socially disruptive deflation.

The euro was a product of the thinking that led to capitalism's untaming in the 1980s and 1990s, when it became an article of faith that monetary policy, managed by a Central Bank, independent of government, was the only feasible tool of economic management. But though that faith has turned out to be spurious, most of the governments of the Eurozone still cling to it—or at least pretend to do so. No one is willing to say out loud that the Eurozone emperor is losing his clothes: that the gamble of Europeanizing monetary policy without Europeanizing fiscal policy has failed. The governments of the weaker economies daren't say so, because they desperately need help from the stronger ones. The governments of the stronger economies won't say so, because if they did, they would have to admit that the logical conclusion is to Europeanize fiscal policy—something they and their predecessors have been running away from for the best part of a generation. They may be able to fudge their way out of the crisis that this conjuncture portends: most of them are dab hands at fudging. But even if they do, the underlying contradiction will still be there. And the supply of fudge is not inexhaustible.

Behind all this looms the specter of renascent nationalisms, echoing the destructive nationalisms of the interwar period and mocking both the supranational hopes of the EU's founders and the subtle blend of social democracy and Christian democracy that has underpinned European governance for sixty years. The specter is particularly noticeable in some (though by no means all) of the former Communist countries of East Central Europe. The savage ethnic conflicts in the former Yugoslavia that I mentioned a moment ago are the most telling example; another is the division of the former Czechoslovakia into two, with a separate, impoverished, and resentful Slovakia confronting a separate Czech Republic. Lesser examples include Poland's far-right Law and Justice Party, led by the notorious Kaczyński twins, the Latvian Fatherland and Freedom Party, and the Europhobic, anti-environmentalist, and ultra-Hayekian Czech president, Václav Klaus.

But renascent nationalism is not confined to the ex-Communist European periphery. It is also a growing factor in some of the member states of the pre-enlargement Union. The United Kingdom is a striking case in point. Britain joined the European Community under a Conservative government. Two years later, in the only nationwide referendum ever held in the United Kingdom, the British voted in favor of Community membership by a majority of two to one. Until the late 1980s, the Conservative Party was more "European" than Labour. But ever since Margaret Thatcher's final phase as prime minister, an increasingly clamant Euro-skepticism has become a central theme of Conservative rhetoric. One reason is that the party leadership is terrified of losing votes to UKIP (the United Kingdom Independence Party), which won 16.5 percent of the total UK vote in the last elections to the European Parliament, more than the governing Labour Party. Though Labour is less Euro-skeptic than the Conservatives, it has effectively abandoned all hope of taking Britain into the euro, for fear of the mystic powers of the tabloid press. Denmark has always been somewhat "Euro-skeptic," partly because Germany has been the "other" for Danish nationalists. Of the big countries of the enlarged EU, Italy and Germany are the least Euro-skeptic. But the Italian Right, which has been in power for most of the last twenty years, is dominated by the crass, fickle media mogul and scandal-haunted populist, Silvio Berlusconi, whose support for the European project is barely skin deep. Even Angela Merkel's Christian Democrats are nothing like as *communautaire* as Helmut Kohl's used to be.

France and the Netherlands are hard to read, but a far-right, essentially nationalist upsurge has plainly taken place in both countries, contributing hugely to the no majorities in the 2005 referendums. In France, the National Front candidate, Jean-Marie Le Pen, came second in the first round of the presidential election in 2002, forcing the Socialist candidate, Lionel Jospin, into third place. Le Pen did much less well in 2007, but he still won almost four million votes. In the Netherlands, the populist and viciously Islamophobic "Party for Freedom," led by Geert Wilders, is the latest manifestation of an ugly combination of racist demagogy and ultra-free-market economics, incarnated, before his assassination, by the gay far-right demagogue, Pim Fortuyn. And the far Right is not confined to France and the Netherlands. Among others, the Northern League and National Alliance in Italy; the Freedom Party in Austria; the British National Party in the United Kingdom; the Flemish Bloc in Belgium; the Popular Party in Portugal; and the People's Party in Denmark all come from the same stable.

These are minorities, but in some countries they are sizeable ones. In any case, the number of far-right voters is only one indicator of the popular mood. Throughout the continent, there is a big pool of resentment—of the ultra-rich, of unemployment and insecurity, of the left intelligentsia, of the political class, of immigrants, and of the EU itself. Far-right parties draw on this pool, but it extends beyond them. The French vote in the Constitutional Treaty referendum was, in large part, a nonideological backlash against headlong enlargement imposed from the top down, without any popular mandate. On the eve of the enlargement, a French public opinion poll showed that 70 percent thought the admission of new members premature, while 53 percent opposed it altogether.[21] During the referendum campaign, the threatening figure of the "Polish plumber" taking jobs away from honest Frenchmen figured largely in anti-Treaty rhetoric. Probably, the same attitudes helped to produce the Dutch result as well. Hubris among the elites had invited nemesis at the hands of the peoples.

So what has gone wrong? Why the disconnect between peoples and elites? Why the failure to discover a common geopolitical vocation and the imbalance between monetary union and fiscal disunion? Why the return of populist nationalism and xenophobia? The answers, I shall argue, lie in the past—ironically in four great ambiguities, without which the successes of the early years would probably not have been achieved. All too often, the price of consensus is fudge, and there was an ample supply of it in the neo-Carolingian empire set up in the 1950s. Ambiguities were everywhere. They were necessary, perhaps inevitable, but they were still ambiguities. This was most obviously true of the fundamentals of ethnicity and identity. The assumptions underpinning the European project were resolutely non-ethnic and implicitly anti-ethnic. Ethnicity was archaic, backward-looking, divisive, and above all, *dangerous*. Unbridled ethnic nationalism had soaked the continent in blood and shame. In the border-less, pacific Europe of the future, Europeans would cherish the supranational ties that united them and forget, or at least downgrade, the ethnic memories that divided them. It was not an accident that Robert Schuman, Alcide de Gasperi, and Konrad Adenauer—the three great political leaders who translated Monnet's vision into reality on the ground—all hailed from the borderlands of their respective countries, about whose ethnic loyalties they were, at best, ambivalent. Schuman was born in the Grand Duchy of Lux-embourg and grew up in Lorraine, then part of the German Empire. De Gasperi was born in the Trentino in northern Italy, then part of the Austro-Hungarian Empire, to whose Parliament he was elected before the First World War. Ade-nauer was famously a francophile, westward-looking Rhine-lander, who cherished a profound suspicion, even loathing, of eastern, militaristic, and as he thought, Nazi-inclined Prus-sia. For all three, transnationalism was second nature.

Personal predilections mattered less than the assumed logic of the integration process. Suffusing the whole project was an essentially teleological understanding of modernity, reminiscent of the teleologies of Bolshevik Russia on the one hand and of theorists of the managerial revolution, such as the former Trotskyite James Burnham in the United States. According to this, small units were bound to give way to big ones, and big ones to ones that were bigger still. The sov-ereign nation-states posited by the Treaty of Westphalia at the end of the Thirty Years' War had subsumed the local or provincial loyalties of the Middle Ages and the early-modern period. Burgundians, Occitans, and Bretons had become Frenchmen; Bavarians, Hessians, and Saxons, Germans. Now it was the turn of a wider European entity to subsume the Westphalian states that made it up.

Of course, national identities and loyalties would continue to exist. (After all, provincial identities and loyalties still existed within the carapace of the Westphalian nation-state.) But they would be survivals of an earlier, backward stage of history, with diminishing emotional force and mobilizing power. Above all, the demons of ethnic nationalism would drown in the warm bath of Europeanism. Indeed, for some of the architects of the European project, even Europeanism was only a stage on the road to something even grander. In the final page of his memoirs, Jean Monnet summed up his vision in a lapidary phrase. The nation-states of the past, he wrote, could no longer resolve the problems of the present. And he added: "The Community itself is only a step towards the forms of organisation of the world of tomorrow."[22] Yesterday, the nation; today, Europe; tomorrow, the world.

Given all this, it is not surprising that the promoters of the European project did not examine, or even think seriously about, the relationship between the new Europe they sought and the old ethnic identities they wanted to get away from. Why awaken sleeping ethnic dogs? Besides, most of the European nation-states that were the original building blocks of the Community were by now fairly (though only fairly) homogeneous ethnically. Thanks to railways radiating out from Paris, to schoolmasters imbued with a uniform, republican ethic, and most of all to universal compulsory military service, the once-profound linguistic and cultural differences between the ancient provinces of France faded almost to vanishing point under the Third Republic. True, France's ethnic homogeneity was complicated by the presence of significant numbers of fairly recent immigrants, to say nothing of the fact that when the European project was launched, Algeria was constitutionally part of metropolitan France. But the complications seemed trivial, at any rate, to French elites.

The same was true of the Netherlands and Federal Germany, and to a lesser extent of Italy. Belgium, divided between French-speaking Walloons in the south and Dutch-speaking Flemings in the north, was the one great exception. But in the halcyon days when the Rome Treaty was signed, even that difference seemed trivial. And so the European project ignored ethnicity. "Europe" was assumed to consist of more-or-less ethnically pure nation-states that shared a common "European" identity and allegiance.

However, the founding fathers said little about the nature of that identity. They approached their task in the spirit of Gertrude Stein: Europe was Europe was Europe. The preamble to the Paris Treaty setting up the Coal and Steel Community spoke of the "contribution which an organised and vital Europe can make to civilisation"; the Rome Treaty spoke of preserving and strengthening "peace and liberty." Peeping between the lines of both texts was the assumption that Europe was more than a geographical expression: that Europeans shared a special vocation, springing from a common civilization and history. But that assumption was implicit, not explicit. Under the circumstances, that was probably inevitable. The founders knew (more or less) what they meant; they saw no need to spell it out. In any case, here as elsewhere, a certain ambiguity was the price of success. The six founder nations of the Community all understood themselves as European and—albeit with reservations in some cases—they also understood each other as European. Had their leaders tried to probe the inner meaning of that understanding, they might have derailed the whole process in a welter of fruitless contention. Better to leave well alone.

Schuman, de Gasperi, and Adenauer were all Catholics—the first two devoutly so. For all of them, Europe had a spiritual dimension as well as mundane ones. But though the Christian Democratic parties they led were indispensable to the creation and development of the Community,[23] they knew that the enterprise could not be exclusively Christian Democratic or even Christian. The same applied to the powerful anticlerical and secularist tradition that permeated French radicalism and socialism. Occasional attempts to define Europe's identity in religious terms failed miserably. No one even tried to define it in secularist terms. It was the same story with political ideology. In what came to be known, not very elegantly, as the "European construction," the two great political traditions of postwar Europe—Christian democracy and social democracy—were joined at the hip. The Belgian socialist Henri Spaak also had a place in the founders' pantheon—only one degree less elevated than those of the great Christian Democratic trio. Guy Mollet, the French prime minister when the Rome Treaty was signed, was another socialist.

The European social model was the child of both the Christian Democratic and the social democratic traditions. So were the mood, style, and tacit ideology of the Community's institutions, most notably of the European Commission. (That was why Margaret Thatcher, the child of an utterly different and uniquely English tradition, viewed it with a mixture of loathing and fear.) But this consensus provided, at most, an incomplete answer to the question "What does it mean to be European?" It showed that the murderous ideological passions of the past had faded along with the even more murderous ethnic hatreds, and that hardly anyone wanted to revive them. The Europe it sustained offered its citizens peace, prosperity, and a better approximation to social justice than they had ever enjoyed before. It also offered the world a model of sober, enlightened, consensual, and postnational rule. These were not small achievements, particularly when set against Europe's past history.

But though the Europe of the consensus was worthy and even inspiring, it was just a little dull. There was plenty of drama in the national politics of postwar Europe—the fall of the French Fourth Republic and the creation of the Fifth, Margaret Thatcher's long and stormy reign in Britain, the demise of Fascism in Portugal and Spain, Willy Brandt's *ostpolitik* in Germany and the eventual fall of the Berlin Wall, to mention only a few examples. The Community's politics, on the other hand, were ostentatiously undramatic. Its processes were opaque and, for most Europeans, mind-numbingly tedious.

It acquired a splendid flag and a soul-stirring anthem (Beethoven's setting of the "Ode to Joy" in the last movement of his Ninth Symphony). But it was hard to translate Beethoven's magnificent evocation of the ideals of freedom, peace, and solidarity into the gnarled jargon of everyday Community life. Europeans of all kinds and degrees learned the Community habits of cooperation, mutual toleration, deal making, and consensus building. These were habits of the intellect and sometimes of the wallet, however, rather than of the heart. The vision they embodied was of Europe as a vast shopping mall, dedicated to an ideal of bourgeois contentment and ever-advancing prosperity. It was a vision for the boom of the 1990s and 2000s. Whether it will suffice for the bust is not so clear.

Another haze of ambiguity enveloped the great questions of how the Community, and later the Union, would be governed. The European project was supposed to transcend national sovereignty. But how far and fast would transcendence go? And whose sovereignties would be transcended? From the first, two visions were in contention; and from the first, the differences between them were fudged. In its official communiqué explaining the Schuman Plan, the French government said in so many words that it would lay the foundation for "the European federation which is indispensable to the preservation of peace."[24] When he assumed his office as the first president of the Coal and Steel Community's High Authority, Jean Monnet declared uncompromisingly that its institutions were "supranational and, let us not shrink from the word, federal."[25] In one of its incarnations, the abortive plan for a European Defence Community would have entailed a big step toward federalism, in the shape of a single European defense minister.

In some quarters, the federalist flame burned on, even after the death of the EDC. After his retirement in 1955, Monnet set up an unofficial "Action Committee for the United States of Europe," to which he devoted the last twenty years of his life. Walter Hallstein, the first president of the European Commission established by the Rome Treaty, was an avowed federalist. The goal was a political union, he insisted, and political union amounted to federation. There was no way of telling when it would be reached, but the "inescapable logic" of economic integration was driving steadily toward it.[26]

Perhaps unconsciously, Hallstein echoed an indigestible body of social science theory, known as "neo-functionalism." Neo-functionalists saw integration as a cumulative process spreading, like an inkblot, from one policy area to the next. First, a common market in coal and steel; then common investment policies in those sectors; then a common market in industrial goods generally; then common economic policies; later, common defense and foreign policies; later still, political union—each step would follow logically from the last. There was no need to debate the nature of the final step or to chart the likely course of its arrival. All that could be left for later. The British socialist thinker Sidney Webb had once proclaimed that socialism was coming with the "inevitability of gradualism." So it would be with European federalism.

Alas for inkblots. Neo-functionalist theory had no place for heroic leadership. In particular, it had no place for Charles de Gaulle, one of the most redoubtable examples of heroic leadership in postwar European history. De Gaulle saw only too clearly where Hallstein's inescapable logic was going, and he loathed what he saw. For him, eternal France, with all its memories of tribulation and glory, was incarnated in the sovereign French state, the custodian of "yesterday's heritage, today's interests and tomorrow's hopes."[27] There was, and could be, no other focus for the loyalties of the French, and what was true of France was true of all other nations worthy of the name. Charges that de Gaulle was a "bad European" are nonsense. He was as good a European as Monnet or Schuman, but he held a different vision of Europe. He dreamed of a "Europe des patries"—a Europe of nations. That notion too was swathed in ambiguity, but when the Fourth French Republic collapsed and the French people turned to him for salvation, he made it abundantly clear what he meant by it. He did his unrelenting best to stymie further moves toward a federal Europe and to cut Hallstein and his loathed Commission down to size. In the short run, at least, he largely succeeded.

In the longer run, things were more complicated. The decade following de Gaulle's departure from office in 1969 began with a flourish of trumpets when the Community's heads of government adopted the goal of monetary union by 1980. Despite repeated disappointments thereafter, it ended with another flourish, when the European Monetary System was established in 1978. Then came the glory years of proto-federalism, beginning with the Single European Act and culminating in the introduction of the single currency.

But the haze of ambiguity remained in place throughout. In a speech to the European Parliament in January 1990, the then Commission president, the thoughtful and engagingly modest Jacques Delors, famously prophesied that the Commission would one day answer to "the democratic institutions of the future federation."[28] The less than engaging German chancellor, Helmut Kohl, repeatedly called for political union, not least to assuage fears that a reunited Germany would be too powerful for its own and Europe's good. At first sight, the 1992 Maastricht Treaty I mentioned earlier seemed to point in the same direction. As well as charting the course to full monetary union, it gave extra powers to the European Parliament and brought justice and home affairs, together with foreign and security policy, into the Union's ambit. The ghosts of Monnet and Hallstein were entitled to cheer: seemingly, "inescapable logic" had prevailed again.

However, de Gaulle's ghost had much to cheer as well. Monetary union was the last stop on an old road, not the first on a new one. Though the British government refused to admit it, it was a necessary concomitant of the single market. The potentates assembled at Maastricht dealt with new roads in a very different way. The Union's "federalist" institutions, the Commission and the Parliament, were carefully excluded from the Union's new policy domains. There, intergovernmentalism would reign. Sovereign states would negotiate common policies when they could, in the time-honored Westphalian manner. When they could not, they would have to agree to disagree. By the end of the twentieth century, Union governance resembled nothing so much as the two-headed "Pushmi-Pullyu" in Hugh Lofting's Doctor Doolittle stories. Covert federalists pushed; covert confederalists pulled. The result was a kind of stasis, of impenetrable obscurity. It would have been hard to devise a better recipe for bemusing the European public.

Ambiguity over government and authority went hand in hand with ambiguity over territory. There was no doubt about the original Six. They were Europe's heartland—the Europe of Charlemagne; the Europe traversed by the Rhone, the Rhine, and the Po. If they were not European, then no one was. But it was not so clear how far Europe extended beyond its Carolingian core. That steely Cartesian, President de Gaulle, tried to penetrate the veil of ambiguity when the British government headed by Harold Macmillan had the temerity to apply for Community membership in the early 1960s. After long negotiations, he vetoed the application, in a characteristically oracular pronouncement, on the grounds that Britain had a privileged relationship with an extra-European power and was therefore not properly European. But after de Gaulle left the scene, the supply of Cartesians ran out. His veto on British membership was lifted, and nothing more was heard of his skepticism about Britain's Europeanness.

Later enlargements were conducted in a spirit of easygoing goodwill, reflecting political imperatives that seemed compelling to Community governments. Greece, Portugal, and Spain joined after the collapse of their quasi-fascist regimes—in the first two cases, at least, to head off lurches to the far left. Austria, Sweden, and Finland joined when the end of the cold war made their previous neutrality redundant. For all six, what mattered was their willingness to accept the norms of pluralist democracy and to adopt the famous "acquis communitaire"—the mass of Community rules that the existing member states had negotiated between themselves. No one asked awkward questions.

Equally, no one asked whether the borderlands of East Central Europe were European in the same sense as the nations of western Europe, or whether they shared the European allegiance that the states of western Europe were supposed to share. To have done so in the days of the cold war would have been tantamount to legitimizing the division of Europe. In any case, there was no point in asking: they were corralled behind the iron curtain. After the velvet revolutions in East Central Europe and the implosion of the Soviet Union, it was unthinkable to question the European credentials of the former Soviet satellites. In their capitals, the talk was of "rejoining" Europe. In the capitals of the west, they were seen as little sisters, a bit bedraggled perhaps, but flesh of Europe's flesh. They were as European as the French or Germans or Italians. As such, they were morally entitled to EU membership. To deny it to them would be treachery to the European ideal. What possible justification could there be for excluding Prague or Warsaw or Budapest from a Union that included Berlin, Vienna, and Munich?

The former Soviet satellites were scrutinized carefully before receiving the prize of EU entry, but the scrutineers focused on their economic capacities—above all on their ability to develop and sustain competitive markets—not on the intangibles of identity and political culture. No doubt, inevitably. The intangibles were (and are) just that: intangible. There are no checklists for culture. And so enlargement to the east rolled on, fairly slowly at first and then with gathering speed. It was an extraordinary achievement and also a necessary one. But it was risky too—more so than the well-intentioned, if somewhat bossy, Commission officials who pushed enlargement forward dared to realize.

One obvious risk was that the citizens of the existing Union might jib, as the voters in the French and Dutch referendums appear to have done. As we shall see, their views were not taken into account. But there was also a less obvious risk. The European project had now moved into the marches where prewar nationalism had been largely ethnic, where democracy, insofar as it existed at all, had usually been tribal, and where forty years of Communist rule had bequeathed a legacy of mistrust mingled with a kind of defensive egotism. Yet no one paid much attention to the differences of culture and experience that divided the new members both from the old ones and from each other. Nor did many ask if the new entrants had laid *their* demons to rest in the way West Germans had done after the war. Few recalled the strident ethnic assertiveness that had plagued the region between the wars, or wondered if its peoples had come to terms with their sometimes less than inspiring conduct during the Holocaust. Like Topsy in *Uncle Tom's Cabin*, the Union "jest growed." It would have seemed indelicate to ask how its growth would affect the cultural chemistry of the European adventure.

The fourth ambiguity runs through the other three. At the heart of the European project lay an unacknowledged but pervasive ambivalence about *politics*. In transcending the nation-state, the founding fathers were also seeking to transcend—or rather to escape from—the messy, vulgar, clamorous irrationality of political life. Their project was, of course, highly political. Most of them were politicians themselves. The bargaining and compromising that lay at the heart of the Community process were a form of politics. But theirs were the politics of the conference table and the *couloir*, not of the debating chamber or the election meeting. For leaders who had lived through Fascism and Nazism, public politics—popular politics—were tinged with danger. Memories of Hitler's brown shirts and Mussolini's black shirts, of jubilant crowds mobilized by vicious demagogues, of a Gadarene populist rush to perdition, stalked their souls. Sharpening such memories was the more immediate specter of Communism, incarnated, in France and Italy most notably, in powerful mass parties and militant trade unions. Naturally, they wanted popular support, but they were wary of popular engagement.

A slightly furtive strain of technocratic rationalism, going back to the French utopian socialist Henri de Saint-Simon in the early nineteenth century, pointed in the same direction. For Saint-Simon, scientific and industrial elites, not the anarchic masses, were the carriers of socialism. The industrial society of the future would be run by an apolitical alliance of employers, organized labor, industrialists, and technologists. Saint-Simonian rationalism chimed with much older traditions that had been part of the mentality of the French public service for generations; and in the postwar years, it was part of the climate of the times almost everywhere. (The postwar British government's faith in national planning was a characteristic example.) In the Community structure, the politics of the *couloir* were embodied in the nationally rooted Council of Ministers, which took the decisions. The supranational Commission, which made the proposals, embodied, in its own eyes at least, a suprapolitical technical rationality. The founding fathers made a pious nod in the direction of public politics, in the shape of the European Parliament. But the nod was not very convincing.

Of course, much has changed since the early days. The postwar generation has left the stage. Memories of the 1930s and 1940s have faded. The specter of Communism has vanished. The European Parliament is enormously more power-ful than it used to be. Yet life in the Brussels village of Union functionaries, national bureaucrats, and lobbyists of all kinds has changed surprisingly little. The European Pushmi-Pullyu is more imposing than it used to be, but it is still the same animal.

In the last few years, the questions that the architects of the European project swathed in ambiguity have emerged to haunt their successors. Three sets of questions stand out. The first has to do with ethnicity and identity. Having been expelled through the door, ethnicity has returned through the window. While Europe has been integrating, the nation-state has been fragmenting. Ancient ethnicities, such as the Bretons, the Corsicans, the Basques, the Catalans, the Welsh, the Scots, and the Flemings, have challenged the metropoli-tan elites in many (perhaps most) of the Union's superficially homogeneous member states. The elites concerned do their best to pretend that all is well with the states concerned, but the pretense is wearing thin. For years, a fundamental ques-tion has been hovering on the edge of the European agenda: how is Europe to accommodate the renascent, premodern, but also postmodern minority ethnic aspirations that have called the whole notion of the nation-state into question? Immigration from the Third World, mostly from former European colonies—notably from Muslim ones—has raised still harder questions. Here, ethnicity has raised its head in a peculiarly harsh and disorientating way, rendered even harsher and more disorientating by the Iraq War and its ef-fects. Can European cultures accommodate Islam? Can Is-lamic traditions accommodate "European values," whatever these may be? These are now among the most difficult and urgent questions facing the continent.

The second set of questions concerns governance and authority. Though the EU is not a federal state, it has evolved, however haltingly, in an unmistakably federalist direction. But there is an important difference between its trajectory and those of "classic" federations like the United States. Classic federations have started with "high politics" and gradually extended to "low politics." The European project started with low politics, but today "high" political questions are unmistakably on the table. Do Europeans want to hold their own in the emerging new configuration of global power? Can they transcend the stultifying compromise between democracy and technocracy—between federalism and confederalism— that currently prevents the Union from doing so?

The third set of questions is the most baffling of all. It has to do with civilization and territory. Is "Europe" merely a geographical expression, as Count Metternich once said of Italy? If so, where are its geographical limits? If it is more than a geographical expression, as the architects of the European project assumed, what makes it so? What *are* the defining characteristics of European civilization, the special European values that give meaning to the notion of a European ideal? And how far does the Europe that shares these values, the Europe that is more than a geographical expression, extend?

These questions are not new. They have been implicit in the European project from the beginning. But they have been given new urgency by the sweeping changes that have made the old language of "West" and "East" redundant. They provide the themes of my remaining chapters. I turn first to identity and ethnicity.

# -III-

## HATE—AND HOPE

Any kiddie in school can love like a fool,
But hating, my boy, is an art.
—Ogden Nash, quoted in Amartya Sen, *Identity and Violence*, 2006

Drawing inspiration from the cultural, religious and humanist inheritance of Europe. . . .
Convinced that, while remaining proud of their own national identities and history, the peoples of Europe are determined to transcend their former divisions and, united ever more closely, to forge a common destiny,
Convinced that, thus "United in diversity," Europe offers them the best chance of pursuing . . . the great venture which makes of it a special area of human hope.
—From the preamble of the proposed European Constitutional Treaty, 2004

LYING ON MY DESK IN FRONT OF ME as I type is my passport. Its cover is an elegant confection of maroon and gold. "European Union," proclaims the first line, in golden capital letters. Beneath, slightly larger golden capital letters add the words: "United Kingdom of Great Britain and Northern Ireland." Beneath that, also in gold, are the arms of her Britannic Majesty, Queen Elizabeth II, complete with the legendary lion and unicorn. On the first facing page inside, the words "European Union" are repeated. Below them are two lines, translating that term into the two Celtic languages of Great Britain, Welsh and Gaelic. Then come the words "United

67

Kingdom of Great Britain and Northern Ireland"; and below them come, once again, their Welsh and Gaelic equivalents. On the penultimate inside page of the passport, alongside a somewhat unflattering photograph and below my full name, are the portentous words "British Citizen." The message is subtly, I almost said slyly, postmodern. It is also remarkably European. I am, my passport tells me, a British citizen. But that is not all I am. I am also a citizen of the European Union, with certain rights over and above those inherent in British citizenship. Among other things, I am represented in the directly elected European Parliament, as well as in the British House of Commons. And British citizenship itself is a far more complicated matter than it used to be. The three non-English political communities of the United Kingdom—Northern Ireland, Scotland, and Wales— all have their own parliamentary assemblies, with separate executives responsible to them, and substantial powers.

As it happens I live in England, so the only British parliament in which I am represented is the United Kingdom Parliament in Westminster. But if I and my family lived in Wales, where I was born, I would also be represented in the Senedd (Assembly) in Cardiff, and the Welsh Assembly government would be accountable for the quality of my health care and of my grandchildren's education. If I lived in Northern Ireland, I would be governed, not just by the United Kingdom government in London, but by a "power-sharing" executive, made up of representatives from both of the Northern Irish confessional communities, the Protestant majority and the Catholic minority. And though Northern Ireland is part of the territory of the sovereign British state, the government of another sovereign state, the Republic of Ireland, also has a role in its governance.

If this sounds complicated, it is. (As we shall see, these complexities are typical of modern Europe.) They are also recent. For most of its history, the British state has been resolutely unitary; for most of the postwar period, it has been highly centralized. Until the 1970s, only marginalized romantics thought the Scots and Welsh were different enough from the English to justify separate elected assemblies of their own. In Northern Ireland, the Unionist (and Protestant) majority had enjoyed unbroken hegemony since the province acquired a degree of local autonomy following southern Ireland's secession from the United Kingdom in 1921. The Welsh Senedd or Assembly and the Scottish Parliament were brought into existence by statutes of the London Parliament, ratified by popular referendums in Wales and Scotland (but not in England) only a little more than ten years ago. The settlement in Northern Ireland was embodied in the famous "Good Friday Agreement" of 1998, now twelve years old.

The whole package has procured a drastic reconstruction of the British state, with incalculable implications for the future. It is not impossible (though it is still unlikely) that Scotland will secede from the Union altogether in the foreseeable future. In Wales, devolution has fostered the emergence of a self-conscious Welsh nation, with its own comprehensive identity—something that Wales (unlike Scotland) had never known before. The settlement in Northern Ireland seems to have achieved a final answer to the "Irish question," which had been a running sore in the politics of the British archipelago for centuries.

But in Great Britain, the largest of the British Isles, the political forces that secured this reconstruction barely existed forty years ago and did not acquire real weight until the 1980s. And the English, overwhelmingly the majority national community of the United Kingdom, hardly noticed what was going on. It used to be said that the British Empire was acquired in a fit of absence of mind. In England, at least, the same could be said of the devolution statutes that transformed the British state more dramatically than anything since the start of the eighteenth century.

One thing, however, the English did notice. The settlement in Northern Ireland was preceded by some thirty years of exceedingly dirty warfare. In pursuance of the old dream of a united, republican Ireland, the IRA (Irish Republican Army) committed a long series of terrorist atrocities, including an attempt to kill the entire British cabinet that almost succeeded. Protestant paramilitaries responded with atrocities of their own. The British government tried hard to suppress both groups of terrorists by force. Altogether, the death toll reached slightly more than thirty-five hundred (well above the total killed in the 9/11 atrocity in New York). The eventual settlement was a settlement of exhaustion. The IRA slowly and reluctantly realized that they could not unite the island of Ireland by force, against the will of the Protestant majority in the North. The British army and security services slowly came to see that they could not forcibly destroy the IRA or its Protestant counterparts. The two warring sides— three if you include the Protestant paramilitaries—had fought each other to a standstill.

The British story is part of a wider European story. In moments of exaltation, British Euro-skeptics are apt to claim that Britain is the oldest nation-state in Europe. Nothing could be further from the truth. The British state is much younger than the French, Danish, and Portuguese states. It did not exist before 1707, when the English and Scottish states came together in a negotiated union. (They had had the same monarch since 1603, but the union of crowns was not a union of states.) In fact, Britain has always been a multinational state, not a nation-state of the classical kind. The union of 1707 was not a spontaneous emanation of shared nationhood. It was the product of a hardheaded bargain between political leaders seeking political and military advantage. After the union, well-directed bribery and lavish outpourings of propaganda—songs like "Rule Britannia" and "The British Grenadiers" and poems like Walter Scott's "Patriotism" were the most stirring—were needed to embed the fragile new state in the affections of its subjects.

Nor was England a true nation-state. Wales was conquered by the English Crown in obscure medieval struggles and formally annexed to England in the sixteenth century. But it remained culturally, emotionally, and to some degree linguistically separate, and is so still. Not all Welsh people sought political autonomy, but none thought they were English. The reconstruction of the British state in the 1990s was less a voyage of discovery than of rediscovery. Old ethnic communities, long predating the modern era, emerged from beneath the centralizing carapace of the modern state, in the name of difference and *recognition*.[1]

That is the story of state after state in today's Europe. The continent has always been a palimpsest of memories, loyalties, and ways of life; today, the older bottom layers are getting out from under the more recent top ones. In country after country, the superficially homogeneous nation-state of the postwar period has been challenged by premodern ethnic communities, reasserting old identities and demanding new rights. Ancient cultural, political, and sometimes linguistic boundaries that the centralizing states of the modern era blotted out have come back into view, like rocks exposed by an ebbing tide. It is as if the medieval jumble of overlapping jurisdictions and multiple loyalties had revenged itself on the state-builders of the early-modern and modern eras, such as Louis XIV in France, Bismarck in Germany, and Cavour in Italy.[2] The notion that modernity equals uniformity and diversity, backwardness has been stood on its head.

As well as Scots, Welsh people and the Catholic community of Northern Ireland, Basques in northwestern Spain and southwestern France, Galicians in another part of northwestern Spain, Catalans in northeastern Spain, Flemings in northern Belgium, Corsicans in the French island of Corsica, and Lombards in northern Italy have rudely disturbed the metropolitan elites of the once-impervious states of which they are citizens. Slovaks, Bosnians, Croats, Slovenes, and Kosovars in the former Soviet bloc have done the same, much more rudely. In some places, the disturbance has been accompanied by violence and terror, as in Northern Ireland. In parts of the former Yugoslavia, as we saw in the previous chapter, violence has been brutal and genocidal. Western Europe has seen nothing on that scale. However, the extremist Basque nationalists of the ETA (Euskadi Ta Askatugana—"Basque Homeland and Freedom") have carried out car bombings and kidnappings reminiscent of those perpetrated by the IRA, though with fewer deaths. The Corsican Fronte di Liberazione Nazionale di a Corsica (National Front for the Liberation of Corsica) is a somewhat feebler variation on the same theme.

Yet disturbance is not necessarily violent. The Belgian state has been more disturbed than any other in western Europe. It was founded in 1830 as a unitary state, dominated by a French-speaking elite. Brussels, the capital city, was French-speaking too; and French-speaking industrial Wallonia, in the south of the country, was richer and more sophisticated than Flemish-speaking Flanders in the north. But after World War II, the demographic, economic, and political balance shifted in favor of Flanders. The once-poor, humiliated, discriminated-against Flemings were now rich and successful—with plenty of old scores to settle. Bitter conflicts between the two linguistic and ethnic communities eventually led to a drastic reconstruction of the entire Belgian state. It is now officially a federation, boasting a fiendishly complex constitution. The federal government shares powers with "Communities" in certain fields, and with virtually coterminous "Regions" in others. The regions have more autonomy than any others in the EU and more than the states of the United States.[3] In this mélange, as one authority puts it, the "federal entity is little more than an intermediate, almost useless cog between Belgian Regions and EU authorities."[4]

But federalization did not end the conflict between Belgium's two linguistic communities. In the Belgian elections of June 2010, the New Flemish Alliance, which stands for eventual independence for Flanders and an immediate transition from federalism to confederalism, won 27 seats out of 150 in the Chamber of Representatives, making it the largest party. (The Vlaams Belang, another secessionist Flemish party, won 12.) To say that the Belgian state no longer exists would be an exaggeration, but not a gross exaggeration. Yet despite years of bitterness, agitation, and political deadlock, physical violence played no part in this transformation.

Belgium is an extreme case of a common pattern. In the last forty years, all but one of the great states of western Europe have had to accommodate autonomist pressures from below. (Germany, the big exception, has been a federal state ever since her uncertain reappearance on the stage of European politics in 1949, and many of the German Laender have deep roots in Germany's variegated history.) Even France, once the supreme example of the centralist, Westphalian European state, has made a bow toward neo-medieval diversity.

Between the central state and the departments created during the revolution there is an elected regional tier of government, armed with tax-raising powers. Among the twenty-one regions of metropolitan France lurk the ghosts of medieval and early-modern duchies like Acquitaine, Auvergne, Brittany, Burgundy, Lorraine, and Normandy, evoking a long history of provincial diversity that the central French state tried unsuccessfully to expunge from popular memories.[5]

Spain, another highly centralist state for most of the last 250 years, has traveled further in the same direction. Following the death of its aged Fascist ruler, Francisco Franco, in 1975, a new democratic constitution declared the Spanish nation to be "indissoluble" but guaranteed its "nationalities" and "regions" a right to self-government. The end result was a wonderfully subtle process of rolling, asymmetric devolution. The "historic" nationalities of Andalusia, Catalonia, Galicia, the Basque country, and (eventually) Valencia enjoyed more autonomy than did the other twelve regions, and gained it more quickly. But the differences between the historic and the nonhistoric were slowly whittled away. All seventeen regions (known as "autonomous communities") have their own legislatures, presidents, governments, administrations, and high courts of justice. Spain is not quite a federation, but the differentiated, fuzzy, and indeterminate pattern of territorial government is closer to federalism than to the centralism of the past.[6] (It also has something in common with the indeterminate pattern of the Middle Ages when the Iberian Peninsula was ruled by a variety of Muslim emirs and Christian princelings.) Here too the politics of diversity and recognition have triumphed over the politics of uniformity and order.

The Italian story has something in common with the Spanish, but it is darker and more poignant. After Italy's unification in the mid-nineteenth century, its rulers sought to mimic the centralist structure of Napoleonic France. "Having made Italy," they hubristically proclaimed, "we must now make Italians."[7] Between the two world wars, Mussolini's Fascist regime governed in the same spirit, only more so. But Italy was too diverse, geographically, economically, and culturally for achievement to match aspiration. After World War II, a new republican constitution provided for directly elected regional governments. Five "special" regions acquired such governments early in the postwar period; fifteen "ordinary" regions, covering the rest of the country, followed suit in the 1970s.

But that was far from the end of the affair. In the early 1990s the postwar republic—commonly known as the "first republic"—collapsed in a welter of corruption and scandal. In the "second republic," the populist, antitax, anti-immigrant, Euro-skeptic, and increasingly Islamophobic Northern League (Lega Nord) has become an ominous presence in national politics. Sometimes the League campaigns for a federal constitution, sometimes for the outright secession of "Padania" (in effect, the north of the country) from the Italian state and its allegedly sponging, wastrel clients in the south. In both guises, as the UCLA historian Perry Anderson puts it, the League is "an insurgent movement," powered by resentment of high taxes, of the polished euphemisms of the political elite, and—increasingly—of immigration. Its forte is "raucous, hell-raising protest," tinged increasingly with "racism and prejudice against Islam."[8]

No neat generalization can capture the complexities of these unexpected turns toward an ethnically and culturally diverse medievalism. The Vlaams Belang in Flanders and the Lega Nord in the Italian North are far-right populist parties, oozing resentment of established authorities of all kinds, particularly those of the European Union, and holding rigid and intolerant visions of the identities to which they appeal. In Spain and France, regionalism was favored by the political left and opposed by the right—though under the Third and Fourth French Republics, the left was still in thrall to the fierce centralism that the Jacobins had championed during the French Revolution. The SNP (Scottish National Party) and Plaid Cymru (Party of Wales) are social democratic in ideology and pro-European in sympathy.

By the same token, the central states created in the modern era have handled neo-medieval, autonomist pressures from below with varying degrees of understanding and skill. The Spanish state has rolled elegantly with the punch; the French state has been more reserved, though still fairly accommodating; the Italian state has floundered; and the British state has shifted from staunch and unyielding unionism to breathtaking devolutionary radicalism in the country's non-English periphery, combined with ferocious centralism in England. Collectively, the EU member states have given a cautious nod to regionalism. A Regional Development Fund to support poorer regions was set up in the 1970s. The Maastricht Treaty established an advisory Committee of the Regions and enshrined the principle of "subsidiarity"—a doctrine derived from Catholic social teaching which holds that decisions should be taken at the lowest feasible level of government—in the Union's informal constitution. Since then, transnational cooperation between regions has grown apace, not least between the coastal fringe of southeast England and the Pas de Calais.

Despite the varied responses of the states affected by them, all these examples of neo-medieval pluralism have challenged the moral and ideological foundations of the

European state system at a peculiarly sensitive point. The classical, Westphalian state claims to embody "the" nation. Packed into that claim is the assumption that *the nation* and *the people* are one and the same. On it rests the further, more far-reaching claim that the sovereign nation-state is the supreme political expression of the sovereign people—that its will is the people's will and its voice the people's voice. But if the boundaries of the same state contain several peoples, not one—if the very notion of *the people* and *the nation* are out of joint with an infinitely more complex reality—then all of these claims collapse. And thanks to the rebirth of medieval pluralism, that is what has happened in state after state in postmodern Europe. One of the most crucial assumptions of the EU's founding fathers was that the ethnically homogeneous nation-state was destined to be the fundamental building block of a supra-ethnic united Europe. Now it looks less like a block than a squashy blob of mud.

The allegedly national states of Europe still exist, within their postwar frontiers. Theirs is still the determining voice in European legislation. They appoint the members of the supranational European Commission and the judges who sit on the European Court of Justice. France and Britain possess nuclear weapons and are permanent members of the UN Security Council. The member states of the Union still enjoy what Max Weber took to be the most essential attribute of statehood—a monopoly of the legitimate use of force. But beneath these imposing trappings lurks a diminished and bewildered manikin, rather like the Wizard of Oz in L. Frank Baum's immortal fable.

There was always an element of bluff in the Westphalian states of Europe. They were products of artifice, will, the accidents of dynastic marriage and the fortunes of war rather than of mystic chords of popular feeling. But for the marriage between James IV of Scotland and Margaret Tudor, daughter of King Henry VII of England, Margaret's grandson, James VI of Scotland, would not have inherited the English Crown, and the British state might never have come into existence. Had Austria defeated Prussia at the battle of Königgrätz, instead of the other way around, there would have been no German Empire, no Third Reich, and probably no German Federal Republic. Had the duke of Burgundy, Charles the Bold, beaten off the depredations of the French Crown in the fifteenth century, a powerful Burgundian state might still exist, dwarfing a puny France.

Europe's nation-states were formed by war, for war. Their armies (and, in Britain's case, navy) were the prime instruments of nation building. But their imposing monuments and patriotic anthems concealed murky pasts, replete with land-grabs and discrimination against ethnic minorities. The eighteenth-century gang rape of Poland by Russia, Prussia, and Austria; the brutal, long-drawn-out British attempt to destroy the culture of the native Irish; and Napoleon III's casual annexation of Nice and Savoy are only three examples of many. The upheavals of the last thirty years have called the perpetrators' bluff. Modernity has gone back on its tracks; the Wizard of Oz has been exposed as a fraud. Not only have premodern ethnic differences refused to lie down and die, but the onward march of integration has given them a new lease on life. As the national boundaries of the last two centuries have become less prominent, and as the threat of war on the European continent has evaporated, the always-artificial nation-states of Europe have begun to unravel, along fault lines inherited from the premodern past. The fault lines may or may not be ethnic in character (though some of them patently are). The crucial point is that they evoke memories and loyalties that modernist metropolitan elites once pooh-poohed, and that they do so because the postmodern and the premodern have turned out to be brothers beneath the skin.

In its early stages, European integration helped to rebuild the power and legitimacy of the states that took part in it. Now that process has gone into reverse. Not only have state borders in Europe's heartland become more porous, but the onward march of integration has constrained the states' freedom of action more and more tightly. An emblematic moment came in 1983. Appropriately, it came in France, the crucible of the European project in the early days and still the core state of the European heartland. Only two years before, François Mitterrand, the wily leader of the French Socialist Party, had won the presidency on a far-left program combining economic dirigisme, extensive nationalization, and Keynesian pump priming. The result was a flight of capital that could have been ended only by autarchic measures incompatible with the rules of the common market and the recently established European Monetary System. The Mitterrand government had to choose between the socialist commitments it had made in the election and its cherished European vocation. After fierce battles between different socialist factions, it chose the latter and abandoned the program on which it had been returned to power.[9]

Nothing as dramatic has been seen since, but that is because the economies of the member states have become so intertwined that over a vast range of policy areas, national administrations are no more than agents of European decision makers—including, of course, themselves. No one forces member governments to comply with European decisions;

the EU has no gunboats. But voluntary compliance is "endlessly renewed on each occasion of subordination."[10] At the same time, the onward march of globalization—both motor and product of capitalism's untaming—has elevated markets and diminished states in Europe, even more than in North America and east and south Asia.

The Westphalian states of Europe are subject to three disorientating sets of pressures—to those of neo-medieval provincialism from below, and to those of Europeanization and globalization from above. The national loyalties and identities that used to sustain them have lost much of their old purchase—and the more purchase they lose, the more difficult it is for the states concerned to resist further losses. The "enfants de la patrie" (children of the fatherland) addressed in the opening line of that most glorious of national anthems, "La Marsellaise," have discovered—or rediscovered—that they are not just "enfants de la patrie" but also of the province, region, county, or city. More important, they have also discovered that the "patrie" is no longer able to protect them from the vicissitudes of the global marketplace and that the price of protection by European authorities is less freedom of action for national ones.

But the state's loss is not Europe's gain: after all, the states collectively *are* Europe. The humbled, weakened, pressured, and often bewildered European states of the twenty-first century have become more, not less, anxious to cling to the prerogatives that remain to them and more, not less, determined to pretend that they are still as powerful and legitimate as they used to be. Like an aristocratic family that has come down in the world, they still insist on wearing the increasingly bedraggled furs and living in the crumbling mansions handed down to them by their ancestors. They are, in short, in denial; and, as people in denial often do, they have become tense, rigid, deceitful, and irrationally defensive.

A nice phrase by the British political scientist Anand Menon has captured one manifestation of their denial. The EU, he suggests, is prey to a "paradox of politics." Member governments pass the buck for unpopular decisions, including decisions they support and for which they have voted, to a remote and menacing entity known as "Europe," while taking the credit for popular ones.[11] On the whole, the tedious, humdrum, but essential business of Union decision making proceeds fairly smoothly. Compromises are reached; give-and-take prevails. The atmosphere is that of a club. There are club bores, but no one pays much attention to them: in her later years as Britain's prime minister, Margaret Thatcher was a club bore *in excelsis*, but she achieved little for her pains. (François Mitterrand's notorious semi-compliment, that she had "the eyes of Caligula and the mouth of Marilyn Monroe,"[12] testified to his susceptibility rather than to her persuasive powers.) Aggressive table banging wins few friends and many enemies. Yet when the national politicians who make up the club speak to their domestic audiences through their domestic media, they depict its business as a series of jousts, with themselves as victorious heroes vanquishing foreign foes.

Another manifestation of the same syndrome is former prime minister Gordon Brown's repeated attempts to smother Scottish and Welsh nationalism with a defensive and profoundly unhistorical rhetoric of what he calls "Britishness." His speeches on that theme were erudite, eloquent, and deeply felt. Yet no one listening to them would have realized that the history of the Britannic isles has been inextricably intertwined with that of the European mainland for

two thousand years and more. A far more damaging manifestation is the contradiction at the heart of the Eurozone
that I discussed in the previous chapter. Any half-competent
economist could have foreseen that the combination of national control over taxation and public spending with a European currency and central bank with would end in tears,
and many did so. But member governments refused to act
on the obvious conclusion that monetary union implied at
least a degree of fiscal union: that would have been an open,
public, and therefore humiliating surrender of the trappings
of sovereignty. Instead, they plunged on, with a kind of hubristic insouciance. So far, they have escaped nemesis. But,
in the face of the Greek debt crisis in the summer of 2010
and the accompanying convulsions in the Eurozone, only the
very brave (or very foolhardy) would be willing to bet that
nemesis will never come.

Against that background, the renaissance of often xeno-
phobic nationalism discussed in the previous chapter falls
into place. It is fueled by resentment, particularly among
the victims of economic change, directed against the political class in general, against the supposedly remote Europhile
elites, and against immigrants. But that is not the whole
story. The combination of premodern provincialism with
postmodern globalization and Europeanization has fueled
a moral crisis—a crisis of identity, meaning, and purpose.
Weakened and defensive states, terrified of losing such prerogatives as remain to them, are not alone in feeling its effect.
So do some (though not all) of the peoples for whom they
claim to speak. Not only have the states grown more assertive
and rigid in response to their loss of capacity and legitimacy;
as the peoples have come to feel that power has slipped away
from the political communities to which they belong, they

have sought scapegoats both at the top of the social pyramid and at the bottom.

Yet the peoples, like the states, are Janus-faced. Xenophobia goes hand in hand with xenophilia. Europe's national differences are far shallower than they were in the early postwar period, let alone in the preceding one hundred years. For most Europeans, particularly in the heartland states of the European mainland, "Europe" is simply a fact of life: no more, but also no less. It is not something to die for, as Euroskeptics often point out. But in the skeletal "market states" of the twenty-first century,[13] it is far from clear that many people are willing to die for their nations either: the great conscript armies that helped to build the nation-states of old days have been replaced with professional, mercenary forces, for which soldiering is a job like any other. Robert Kagan's famous jibe that Americans are from Mars, but Europeans from Venus, contains an element of truth.

Ironically, however, the American public's reaction to the dragging Iraq and Afghanistan wars has shown that most of Kagan's fellow countrymen are also from Venus rather than Mars. Americans were happy to applaud the quick and crushing victory over Saddam Hussein at the start of the Iraq War. They have been markedly less enthusiastic about the long-drawn-out conflicts in distant places that have followed, in which American boys have been killed for increasingly unglamorous and incomprehensible causes.

Some time ago, the British sociologist A. D. Smith pointed out that there is no European equivalent of "Armistice Day, no European ceremony for the fallen in battle."[14] He failed to add that the national ceremonies no longer carry the emotional charge that they once did. "Dulce et decorum est pro patria mori," wrote the Roman poet Horace. ("It is sweet and fitting to die for one's country.") The sentiment has few takers today. The European continent is full of the iconography of death in battle. Sometimes it brings a lump to the throat. Perhaps the most poignant examples are the memorials to the dead of the First World War, bearing the haunting inscription "Morts pour la France" (Dead for France), which visitors find in village after village in the French provinces. But one weeps (or almost weeps) for the young men killed before their time, and for the families who mourned them; the ties of nationhood are unaffected.

In the civilian states of today, dying is no longer the point. Even more than in the past, identity is not monolithic or unidimensional. Postmodern Europe is a rich soup of fluid, shifting identities, sometimes reinforcing each other and sometimes cross-cutting or even colliding. Some are chosen, some are fated. Some were pressed into service by the states that took part in the terrible European civil wars of the last one hundred years; others were not. They cannot be forced into a permanent hierarchy of emotional significance or historical importance. Karl Marx thought class identities—or at least the class identity of the proletariat—trumped national ones. It turned out, not just that the workers *did* have fatherlands, but that they were prepared to fight for their fatherlands against other workers with different ones. Some feminists talk as if gender identities trump all others, but few women seem to agree with them.

Exactly the same is true of the great prophets of nationhood, and for that matter of the less clamant prophets of a superordinate European identity—and even of some of the champions of the reborn medievalism of our time. Nationalists assumed that national identities were supreme and all-encompassing. Europeanists thought that petty national identities would gradually be subsumed by a greater European identity. Occasionally, neo-medievalists talk as if the ties of the local and the familiar are the only ones that matter. But a moment's thought will show that these simplicities are nonsensical. It is perfectly possible to be European *and* British *and* Welsh—*and* a wine drinker, thriller lover, pensioner, theatergoer, grandparent, ex–university teacher, and member of the male sex. I should know: I am all of these things myself. Context is all. I realized I was European when I spent a year as a graduate student in California. Now the fragmentation of the British state is encouraging me to rediscover my Welsh roots. My story is commonplace in twenty-first-century Europe.

More challenging to the European project than the resurrection of the old ethnicities of province and locality are the new dilemmas posed by immigration from former European colonies in the Third World, and above all from the Islamic world. Muslim immigrants helped to satisfy western Europe's voracious appetite for cheap and unskilled labor during the long boom of the mid-twentieth century. The immigrants were wretchedly poor, miserably housed, and subject to humiliating discrimination, but they were too weak politically and too ill-equipped educationally to protest effectively. In any case, they did not particularly want to protest: they were better off, in most ways, than they had been in their home countries. For all practical purposes, they were invisible.

But they did not remain so. Contrary to expectations, they stayed in Europe. They had children, born on European soil, and speaking European languages, in local accents. They also had a culture, or rather cultures. Mosques sprang up in Muslim areas, often replacing derelict Christian churches.

Imams were imported from Islamic countries. Halal butchers appeared on European streets; Bangladeshi, Moroccan, and Turkish cuisine titillated British, French, Dutch, and German taste buds. In European city after European city there were Muslim quarters, closer in atmosphere to North Africa or the Middle East or South Asia or Indonesia than to the non-Muslim quarters. But though the Muslim population became more visible, the second, European-born generation still faced invisible barriers of prejudice and incomprehension that kept them out of full membership of the European societies to which, in theory, they belonged. Most got on with their lives as well as they could. Some nursed psychic wounds of resentment and alienation. A handful gave way to murderous rage.

The Muslim presence in contemporary Europe bulks larger in European (and American) imaginations than in fact. As a proportion of the total EU population, the Muslim population is certainly significant, but it is far from overwhelming. In 2003, the Muslim share of the total population of the then fifteen EU member states was around 4 percent. If the new members that have joined in the last decade and the candidate members in the western Balkans are added in, the Muslim proportion rises to around 4.6 percent. But in certain EU member states, the proportion is much higher. In France, it is between 8 percent and 10 percent; in the Netherlands, a little more than 6 percent. In some urban concentrations, the proportion is very much higher. In the United Kingdom, the Muslim proportion of the total population is less than 3 percent, but in the London borough of Tower Hamlets, it is 36 percent. In Marseilles it is 25 percent, in Amsterdam 24 percent.[15] And Muslim birthrates are higher than the non-Muslim average, while non-Muslim populations are falling.

The result is a kind of moral panic in parts of the indigenous population. Examples are legion. One of the most highly charged was the so-called Rushdie affair in Britain. In 1988 Salman Rushdie, a lapsed Muslim born in Bombay but educated in a prestigious British boarding school, published an extraordinary, in places haunting, novel, *The Satanic Verses*. It lampooned both the Prophet Muhammad, for Muslims the messenger of God, and the Qur'an, the word of God. It also exhumed an ancient story to the effect that certain Qur'anic verses were written by Satan—a story that undermines the crucial Muslim belief that the Qur'an was dictated to Muhammad by God. It provoked an explosion of outrage among Muslims, first in Britain but eventually worldwide.

*The Satanic Verses* was burned in the northern English city of Bradford, banned in most Muslim countries, and provoked the Ayatollah Khomeini, the leader of Iran, into issuing a *fatwa* ordering Rushdie's death. Bookshops alleged to be stocking *The Satanic Verses* were firebombed. Rushdie's Japanese translator was stabbed to death; the Italian translator was seriously wounded. Rushdie went into hiding. In May 1989 London was the scene of an anti-Rushdie march, vividly depicted by the historian and writer Malise Ruthven. The marchers, he wrote, "wore white hats and long baggy trousers with flapping shirt tails. Most of them were bearded; the older men looked wild and scraggy with curly, grey-flecked beards." After decades in Britain, "they still seemed utterly *foreign* . . . irredeemably provincial."[16]

Not only did they seem provincial, but to British secular liberals, they also seemed fanatical, bigoted, and threatening. For they were not marching against poverty, deprivation, social injustice, or even racial prejudice and discrimination: that, secular liberals would have applauded. They were marching against insults to their faith and assaults on their community and their honor—a concept without meaning in the secular, hedonistic societies of our time. Almost without exception, secular liberals rallied to Rushdie and the cause of free speech, shades of Voltaire hovering in the background. Two absolutisms were in conflict: the Islamic absolutism of the marchers and the secularist absolutism of the liberal intelligentsia, to which Rushdie himself belonged.

The Rushdie affair was the first premonitory rumble of a storm that shows no sign of abating. Across the Channel, the French state has been embroiled in a long-running conflict with sections of the Muslim community in the name of the republican tradition of *laïcité*—a term with no real English equivalent, meaning, in effect, not just the separation of church and state as in America, but the relegation of religion to the private sphere and its rigorous exclusion from the public. A commission set up by President Chirac in 2003 inquired into the growing tendency of Muslim girls to wear head scarves while at school. It concluded that most of them had been pressured into doing so by (male) relatives and recommended that head scarves—along with Jewish yarmulkes and "large" Christian crosses—should be banned from state schools. In 2004 a new law was passed doing just that.

But the saga went on. In a state of the nation address five years later, Chirac's successor, the brash populist Nicolas Sarkozy, declared that the "burqa," a full-body covering worn mainly by women in Afghanistan, was "not welcome in France." The burqa, Sarkozy explained, was "not a religious symbol, but a sign of subservience and debasement." The applause from listening parliamentarians was "raucous."[17] No one seems to have asked what qualified him and his followers to pronounce on the symbols of a faith they did not share; in July 2010 the French Parliament launched a debate on a proposal to make it illegal to wear the burqa anywhere in public. Not for the first time in French history, the republican tradition had revealed a distinctly monarchical face.

However, the harshest attacks on Muslim values and sensibilities, and the most ferocious explosions of Muslim rage, have taken place in the once-sedate and buttoned-up Protestant cultures of northern Europe. Emblematic examples were the Amsterdam murder of the Dutch filmmaker Theo Van Gogh in 2004, and its contorted prelude. Van Gogh was a neurotic, driven, and loutish misfit who delighted in aggressive provocation of all and sundry. Jews had taken him to court for obscene anti-Semitic tirades, Christians for calling Christ a "rotten fish." Then came his notorious film, *Submission*, scripted by Ayaan Hirsi Ali, a Mogadishu-born renegade Muslim woman who had become a passionate campaigner against the faith in which she had been brought up. Qur'anic verses, demanding female submission to male relatives, were projected onto the skins of naked women who were supposedly telling Allah their stories of abuse and rape. Two months later, Van Gogh was shot dead in the street by another neurotic misfit, an Islamist extremist called Mohammed Bouyeri. After shooting him eight times, Bouyeri proceeded to cut Van Gogh's throat, almost decapitating him, and then stabbed him in the chest. There followed a number of arson attacks on mosques and Islamic schools, and a smaller number of similar attacks on churches.[18] Since then, the far-right, harshly Islamophobic Party of Freedom, led by the egregious Geert Wilders, has steadily gained ground. In the national elections of 2006, it won just under 6 percent of the vote. In the European Parliament election three years later, it won 17 percent.

Hard on the heels of the Van Gogh murder came the notorious affair of the Danish cartoons lampooning the prophet Muhammad, in one case as a bomb-throwing terrorist. The right-wing newspaper *Jyllands-Posten* published the cartoons in 2005. The paper's culture editor explained, in horrified tones, that "modern secular society is rejected by some Muslims." The paper's purpose, he added, tongue massively in cheek, was to "integrate" Muslims "into the Danish tradition of satire."[19] The results included a wave of protest across the Islamic world, eagerly ramped up by assorted Danish imams; the torching of a number of Danish embassies; death threats against the cartoonists; and a Muslim boycott of Danish goods that allegedly cut Denmark's exports to the Middle East by 50 percent between February and June 2006.[20] The chief beneficiaries of the affair were Islamic radicals on the one hand and populist European Islamophobes on the other.

Violent disturbances in heavily Muslim areas, such as parts of Oldham, Leeds, and Bradford in the north of England, of Lille and Arras in northeastern France, of Marseilles on France's Mediterranean coast, in the notorious *banlieues* of Paris and in run-down central Brussels, were an ominous counterpoint. Equally ominous was the savage public reaction when Dr. Rowan Williams, the archbishop of Canterbury and spiritual head of the worldwide Anglican communion, had the temerity to explore the relationship between Islamic religious law (or *Sharia*) and the law of the land, in a secular state. Williams's discussion of these issues was thoughtful, learned, and subtle; despite its modest, almost tentative language, it was also challenging—intellectually and politically.

Williams sought to take the debate beyond the dogmatic absolutes of liberal individualism and legal positivism on the one hand and religious fundamentalism on the other, to show that in diverse, pluralistic societies, communal religious legal codes (Orthodox Jewish as well as Muslim) could coexist with an overarching national law. His reward was an extraordinary deluge of vituperation. Needless to say, much of it came from the popular press and the lumpen bullyboys who haunt the blogosphere. But it came from more elevated quarters as well—notably including Prime Minister Brown, a number of lesser government ministers, the two opposition parties, the National Secular Society, certain Muslim leaders, assorted bishops, the chairman of the official Equality and Human Rights Commission, and Williams's predecessor as archbishop of Canterbury, the conservative Lord Carey. If this is not moral panic, it is hard to imagine what would be.

The Islamophobia associated with moral panic is the true twenty-first-century equivalent of the Judaeophobia and eventual anti-Semitism that culminated in the horrors of the twentieth. It is also the greatest single threat to the values and practices of pluralist democracy in Europe. Pockets of anti-Semitism can still be found there, particularly in the ex-Communist "new" Europe beloved of American neocons; throughout the continent, anti-Semitic outrages have multiplied in the aftermath of the Israeli invasion of Gaza in early 2009. But with all its enduring nastiness, anti-Semitism no longer has much political bite. Muslims, not Jews, are the chief targets of far-right parties like the British National Party, the French National Front, and the Danish People's Party, as well as of the Italian Lega Nord and the Flemish Vlaams Belang I discussed a moment ago. In present-day Europe, only tiny numbers could be mobilized behind an overtly anti-Semitic platform. As the previous chapter showed, recent election results make it all too clear that Islamophobia can be a powerful vote winner. The tangled emotions on which it feeds must not be left to fester. They should be exposed to the light of argument and debate.

Islamophobia is, in part, a response to the undoubted threat of Islamist terrorism. The horror of 9/11 was real, after all. So were the Madrid bombings of commuter trains in 2004, Theo Van Gogh's murder, and the London Underground bombings in 2005. Equally, it is true that there has been a turn to radical Islamism on the part of a small minority of alienated and disaffected young Muslim men, usually of the second "immigrant" generation.[21] But this is by no means the whole story. Like Judaeophobia and subsequent anti-Semitism in the nineteenth and twentieth centuries, twenty-first-century Islamophobia has deep roots in Europe's past. In it, old stereotypes, many dating from the days of the Ottoman threat to "Christendom," some from the days when European empires held down Muslim populations, and some from the West-East antimony dating from ancient Greece, have been given a new lease on life.

Thus, Muslims are backward, illiberal, cruel, alien, and depraved. Their societies are "less evolved" than Western ones; their culture is irredeemably hostile to Western cultures; their religion is nothing more than a pretext for male "tom-catting."[22] Because of all this, Muslim civilization "clashes" with Western, Judaeo-Christian civilization in innumerable ways and a host of places. Muslim immigrants to Europe are the advance guard of a civilizational and ultimately political invasion that is turning Europe into "Eurabia" and Europeans into strangers in their own lands.[23] The financial historian Niall Ferguson has warned that "a youthful Muslim society to the south and east of the Mediterranean is poised to colonise—the term is not too strong—a senescent Europe." Conceding that Muslims are a minority in present-day Europe, the journalist Christopher Caldwell has declared that "minorities can shape countries. They can conquer countries." In a bizarre flourish, he added that there are more Muslims in present-day Europe than there were Bolsheviks in prerevolutionary Russia.[24]

To some extent, the fears behind these charges reflect a real phenomenon. Immigrant communities from rural villages, with low literacy rates, little or no knowledge of the languages of the countries to which they have immigrated, little knowledge even of Islamic texts, and with formulaic and highly conservative religious practices, are bound to find it hard to adapt to European cultures—which, in turn, cannot easily make room for them. But the phenomenon is not unprecedented. It has plenty of parallels in other periods of history and other societies. In the nineteenth century and early twentieth centuries, much the same was true of Irish and Polish immigration to the United States, of Irish immigration to Great Britain, and of Jewish immigration both to Western Europe and to the United States from the Russian Pale.

There is more to the moral panic than that. Two tropes run through Islamophobic rhetoric: one broadly political and the second essentially personal. The political trope insists that Islam is quintessentially illiberal and intolerant, and quintessentially un- or even antidemocratic. As such, it is incompatible with the fundamental political commitments of European societies and of the EU itself. It is closed, hegemony-seeking, impermeable to argument and public reasoning, and incapable of taking part in them, whereas European civilization is open, pluralistic, and democratic. At least potentially, European Muslims are also disloyal to and detached from the non-Muslim political communities in which they necessarily live: Muslims owe allegiance to the worldwide Islamic "umma," not to non-Muslim states.

The personal trope echoes that critique, and adds to it. It says that Islam is inherently misogynist—that it discriminates against women in a host of ways, subjects them to degrading practices like clitorectomy and polygamy, imposes forced marriages on them, keeps them out of public space, for example by forcing them to wear the hijab or the burqa, and in general treats them as second-class citizens. And, according to this second trope, misogyny is only the tip of a mighty iceberg of reactionary fundamentalism. Muslims are hostile to gay rights, to freedom of speech and opinion, and more generally to the whole culture of easygoing, permissive individualism that dominates twenty-first-century Europe. They seek to curb the hard-won freedoms that the aging baby boomers of the 1960s boast of having won from their unenlightened parents' and grandparents' generations. They want to go back to the bad old days when gays could not display their sexuality in public, when cohabitation was frowned upon, when it was assumed that marriages would last, and when authority—including religious authority—was respected. The fact is that Islam is incompatible with the libertarian, individualistic civilization of modern Europe and, on a more profound level, with its roots in the Enlightenment.

For better or worse (probably worse), this trope continues, Muslims are here in large numbers, and their numbers will grow rapidly as the century advances. Hardly anyone argues for repatriating them. But they should, indeed must, assimilate into the wider non-Muslim community. They must abandon their Islamic identities and become brown (or brownish) Europeans. Two implications follow. Muslims must accommodate to post-Enlightenment, individualistic secularism as Christians and Jews have allegedly done. They must sunder the communal ties of faith and treat their religion as a marginal, personal matter only, rather like a taste for Chinese food or Mediterranean holidays, with no role in the public sphere. Secondly, the majority society must abandon well-meant but weak-minded theories of multiculturalism, which lead in practice to the appeasement of Muslims and the surrender of crucial aspects of our own Open Societies.

Some of these charges belong to the realm of fantasy. The notion that a vast army of Muslims lurks in North Africa and the Middle East, waiting to colonize Europe, is straightforward paranoia. The parallel between modern European Muslims and Russian Bolsheviks ninety years ago is an example of the higher lunacy. But it would be a mistake to dwell on such examples of the wilder shores of Islamophobia. What matters is its inner core: its fatal misunderstanding of Islam (and other religions) in the first place, and of the notions of identity and multiculturalism in the second. At the heart of Islamophobic rhetoric lies the assumption that Islam is a homogeneous, unchanging monolith, embracing the entire Muslim world, to which all European Muslims necessarily cleave. The truth is that Islam is, if anything, a lot less monolithic than Catholic or Orthodox Christianity, and remarkably heterogeneous. It has no pope, no priests, no church, and no hierarchy. Since the 1920s, it has had no caliph; and even when it had a caliph, his authority was fluctuating and uncertain. The Ottoman caliph, whose empire was allied to Germany and Austria-Hungary in the First World War, tried to foment a holy war against the Allies but failed dismally.

True, the Qur'an is, for Muslims, the unmediated word of God (which is not true of the Jewish or Christian Bibles), but that does not mean it is beyond argument. It is a text; and texts always have to be interpreted. As such they are necessarily open to debate; and the history of Islam has been studded by theological and philosophical controversy. The rigid, puritanical, and intolerant Wahhabi Islam that predominates in most of Saudi Arabia does not embrace the more sophisticated and cosmopolitan coastal area of the Hijaz, where the holy cities of Mecca and Medina are located.[25] As everyone now knows, Sunni Islam differs in a host of ways from the Islam of the Shias, which itself contains at least three different strands. From Islam's earliest days, mystical and ascetic Sufi sects have cut across these divisions.[26] A further complication is that Muslim rulers, like their Christian counterparts, have often manipulated religious groups for their own ends, and that many still do. As a result, local, national differences play at least as large a part in Islam as in Christianity. Turkey and Saudi Arabia are both predominantly Sunni, but Sunni Turks are very different in culture and mentality from Saudi ones.

As for the charge that Islam is inherently un- or anti-democratic, robustly democratic India contains more than 160 million Muslims, who account for more than 13 percent of the total Indian population—a higher proportion than in any existing EU member state apart from Cyprus. (If and when the West Balkan countries join the EU, Albania and Bosnia-Herzegovina will join Cyprus in that respect.) Nor are Muslim identities monolithic and all-encompassing. No identities are. As I argued a moment ago, we all have multiple identities; and we all have to decide how and when different identities trump, or have to negotiate with, others. This is as true of the Ayatollah Khomeini or the suicide bombers of 9/11 as of anyone else. There is nothing intrinsically impossible about being Muslim, part of the worldwide *umma*, and at the same time French and also European—just as there is nothing intrinsically impossible about being a Catholic or an atheist or a Jew and also British and European.

Indeed, many Islamophobic attacks on Muslims are ee-rily reminiscent of attacks that used to be leveled against Jews ("they stick together, they can't be trusted, they put their Jew-ish identities ahead of their national loyalties," and so on). And, in sober fact, the Muslim allegiance to the worldwide Islamic *umma*, insofar as it exists, has a lot in common with the transnational Jewish loyalties of the diaspora, and with the feelings of solidarity that many non-Israeli Jews cher-ish for the state of Israel. Equally, Jewish assimilation into non-Jewish cultures and polities was never an all-or-nothing affair. You could (and can) be a keen cricketer or pétanque player, an enthusiastic football fan and a successful advocate or politician, with large numbers of gentile friends, and at the same time a religious Jew, observing the Jewish dietary code, celebrating Jewish religious festivals, raising your children in the Jewish faith, and regularly attending a synagogue.

In truth, the whole notion of "assimilation" is a blind alley. It is unidirectional, intolerant, and fearful. It assumes that "they," the minority, must become carbon copies of "us" the majority: that "they" must adopt "our" ways and share "our" loyalties. By the same token, it also assumes that "our" ways are better than "theirs," that "we" are more advanced and more sophisticated than "they." It is not racist, as the Nazis were, but it is patronizing and authoritarian. It sees the diversity that has become a hallmark of the postmodern world as a threat, not as a promise, and seeks to hold it at bay. Assimilationists are not necessarily Islamophobes, but they give aid and comfort to Islamophobia. They give a barren an-swer to the wrong question. In a world—and a Europe—in which Islam is the fastest-growing religion, the right question is not how to turn Muslims into brown Europeans. It is how Muslims and non-Muslims can learn to live together, how to create spaces for a growing Muslim minority—which will increasingly consist of European-born EU citizens—within the common European civilization to which they will have as much right to belong and contribute as any other Europeans. By the same token, multiculturalism does not imply that the majority culture "appeases" or should "appease" minority cultures. It insists that different subcultures, within the same overarching political community, should negotiate, argue, debate with, and learn from each other. The charge that European multiculturalism amounts to a sinister kind of civilizational appeasement rests on the premise that "we," the Europeans, children of the Enlightenment, and denizens of Open Societies, have nothing to learn from "them," the unenlightened and incorrigibly closed-minded Muslims. This is a strange kind of counterfundamentalism, a form of illiberal liberalism, as closed-minded and hermetic as the alleged fundamentalism of Islam or the Bible Belt of America.

Peculiarly illiberal is an aggressive secularism, typified by the Oxford biologist Richard Dawkins and the American polemicist Christopher Hitchens.[27] For these and their ilk, religion does not belong in the public sphere at all. Religious leaders, indeed ordinary religious believers, have no right to intrude their faith into public debate. Science has proved that God does not exist. Only the deluded think otherwise. To argue for or against rival public policies on religious grounds is to succumb to cultural primitivism and mental retardation. Believers may practice their religion in private, but they should keep it private.

What aggressive secularists forget is that the notion of a private religion is an oxymoron. Religions are social, not solitary. They are about behavior in this world as well as about the nature of the divine. Their adherents are supposed to bear witness to their faith, and bearing witness is by definition a public act. All this is particularly true of Islam, for which "the transcendent is made manifest in every aspect of daily experience."[28] For aggressive secularists and self-styled "new" humanists, disdain for Islam reflects a generalized disdain for religion as such, but it goes deeper than that. Bewailing the disappearance of the old humanism of his parents, the British philosopher and commentator Roger Scruton notes that instead of idealizing man, the "new humanism" merely "denigrates God"; he is struck, he adds, not only by the "new" humanists' lack of positive belief but by their "need to compensate for this lack by antagonism towards an imagined enemy."[29] It is a perceptive comment, but it does not capture the full meaning of secularist Islamophobia. In Europe, at least, declining Christianity may indeed be an imaginary enemy. Islam is a different matter. Its challenge to the hedonistic instrumentalism and shallow scientism of the age cuts closer to the bone than anything Christianity offers.

Counterfundamentalism of this sort also does violence to the facts of history. It pits a monolithic Islam against a monolithic Enlightenment. Both contestants are imaginary. As I argued a moment ago, Islam is not monolithic. And nor was the Enlightenment. As the distinguished American social and cultural historian Gertrude Himmelfarb has argued, there were several Enlightenments, not one.[30] The rationalistic French Enlightenment of Voltaire and the eighteenth-century *philosophes* was very different from the British Enlightenment, typified by the broad and generous statesmanship of Edmund Burke—champion of the rich diversity of Indian civilization against the misrule of the British East India Company, and defender of Enlightened Europe against the destructive simplicities of the narrowly rationalistic *philosophes*. Different again was the liberty-loving American Enlightenment of Benjamin Franklin and the architects of the United States Constitution.

To fit into a multipolar world, without an East or a West, Europe will have to rediscover its own complex and contested past. It will have to abandon the 2,500-year-old myth that it is itself as monolithically "Western" as Kipling's poem assumed. In truth, Europe has always been "Eastern" as well as "Western." There was a significant Muslim presence in Europe from the days of "Moorish" Spain, or Al-Andalus as its Muslim inhabitants called it, to the eve of the First World War. Al-Andalus was established in the early eighth century CE. By the time the Christian Reconquista of Spain was completed at the end of the fifteenth century, nearly 800 years later, the Ottoman Turks were already installed at the other end of the continent. In the nineteenth century, the Ottoman Empire gradually lost most of its European territories. But it lasted until the end of the First World War and ruled Albania and large parts of Bulgaria and Greece until 1913.

For most of the last 1,300 years, a largely or wholly Muslim polity has embraced at least a part of Europe, albeit a different part at different times. And though the Ottoman contribution to European civilization was not particularly distinguished, Islamic Spain's was extraordinary. In Rosa Menocal's wonderful phrase, Al-Andalus was the "ornament of the world," one of the glittering peaks of a civilization that stretched from the Atlantic to the Himalayas and that helped to illumine a dark and backward Western Europe.[31] "White" Europeans aren't as white as we think, and nor is our continent. For more than 1,200 years, European civilization has carried an "eastern" Muslim imprint. The Bangladeshi quarter in London's East End, or the Moroccan quarter in Amsterdam, are part of a story that was more than a thousand years old when the United States was founded. Bosnian Muslims are as European as Danish Lutherans or French secularists; the great Mosque of Córdoba is as much a part of Europe's cultural heritage as Chartres Cathedral or Shakespeare's sonnets.

Europe's search for its non-"Western" past will be a political process—an aspect of the politics of recognition—as well as a cultural and intellectual one. In a different way, much the same applies to the reborn medievalism of our time, to the increasingly rancid debates over the place of Europe's Muslim minority in a non-Muslim Union, and to the rise of aggressive secularism and illiberal liberalism. The questions at issue go to the heart of the second major theme of this book—the theme of governance and authority. To that I now turn.

# -IV-

## THE REVENGE OF POLITICS

For we alone regard the man who takes no part in public affairs . . . as good for nothing; and we Athenians decide public questions for ourselves or at least endeavour to arrive at a sound understanding of them, in the belief that it is not debate which is a hindrance to action, but rather not to be instructed by debate before the time comes for action.

—Pericles' Funeral Oration, from Thucydides'
*History of the Peloponnesian War*, 431 BCE

*Gregory (Scotland Yard Detective):* Is there any other point to which you would wish to draw my attention?
*Sherlock Holmes:* To the curious incident of the dog in the night-time.
*Gregory:* The dog did nothing in the night-time.
*Holmes:* That was the curious incident.

—Sir Arthur Conan Doyle, "Silver Blaze," 1892

ON 1 DECEMBER 2009, after nearly a decade of confusion and vacillation, the EU's Lisbon Treaty came into force. Like its abortive predecessor, the 2004 Constitutional Treaty, it was designed to counter the centrifugal forces that the admission of twelve new member states had let loose. To some extent, that is what it did. It simplified the Union's cumbersome decision-making process; gave the European Council of EU heads of government a semi-full-time president; and created a new post of High Representative for foreign affairs. At the same time, it increased the powers of the European

102

Parliament; endowed the Union with a single legal personality; and made the EU Charter of Fundamental Rights legally binding (though with opt outs for Britain, Poland, and the Czech Republic).

These changes matter. They have removed some of the obstacles to effective decision making and made it marginally easier for the Union to raise its profile in the outside world. But the key word in that sentence is "marginally." Henry Kissinger's snide question—"If I want to talk to Europe, what number do I call?"—is as pertinent as ever. The Lisbon Treaty was a palliative, or rather a set of palliatives. It did not equip the Union for a world that bears virtually no resemblance to the mental maps its elites and peoples have inherited from their past. It was not intended to. Europe's leaders sought a better way of doing business as usual; the last thing they wanted was a new kind of business. The European Union is still a hobbled giant. The haze of ambiguity that has surrounded its governance since the beginning of the European project is still there. It is still caught in a no-man's-land between federalism and confederalism—and between democracy and technocracy. Its institutions still lack the political legitimacy and moral authority to steer Europe through the shoals of a new century, in which the venerable categories of "East" and "West" have been emptied of meaning. The treaty is a staging post on a journey to a still unknown destination, not the destination itself, an opportunity to take stock and look ahead, not an excuse for dodging the great questions of purpose, principle, and power that now press in on European elites and peoples. Tragically, there has so far been more dodging than looking.

In this chapter, I shall try to redress the balance: to probe the unanswered questions that the European Pushmi-Pullyu has brushed under the carpet. I begin by trying to tease out the inner meaning of the long-drawn-out negotiations that culminated in the Lisbon Treaty's belated ratification. As in the Sherlock Holmes story, their most striking feature was the dog that did not bark in the night. There was no searching *pan-European* public debate about the meaning of the treaties and the political vision that the Union was supposed to incarnate. Vigorous—often bad-tempered—debates took place in some of its member states, but these were national, not European. They focused on the pros and cons for the particular member state concerned; the implications for the Union as a whole were virtually ignored. Opponents dilated on the loss of sovereignty their country would suffer if the proposals went through, supporters on the influence it would lose if it scuppered the project.

The passion, moral seriousness, and philosophical depth of the extraordinary public debate that followed the drafting of the United States Constitution in 1787 and preceded its adoption in 1788 were conspicuous by their absence. No European Alexander Hamilton or James Madison set out the moral values and political assumptions that underpinned the treaties, or defined the ends they were supposed to realize. Words like "virtue," "liberty," and the "public good"—words that reverberated through the American debate—were hardly heard. The moving rhetoric of the *dalit* (once "untouchable") leader B. R. Ambedkar during the parliamentary debates on the Indian Constitution after independence had no European equivalent either.[1] No one explored, as he did, the tension between the democratic promise of political equality and the economic inequality inherent in a market economy; still less did anyone discuss its implications for the European project. Not for the first time, the European public was fobbed off with thin gruel.

The obvious question is, why? It is not a new question. Ten years ago, the Oxford political theorist Larry Siedentop correctly identified James Madison as the most outstanding contributor to the American debate of the 1780s and bewailed the lack of European Madisons.[2] (He said nothing about Ambedkar.) But when Siedentop wrote, the question could be dismissed as airy-fairy academicism. The euro had just been launched, and the great adventure of enlargement to the east was about to begin. The sunlit uplands of perpetual economic growth seemed within reach. America was the world's only superpower and seemed set to remain so. It was not a good time for Cassandras, and Siedentop did not try to be one. His tone was relaxed, conversational, and a little donnish. He wanted Europe to emulate American federalism one day, but he did not think that day would come for decades or even generations.

Things are different now. The time for relaxed academicism is over. The contrast between the vigorous and often profound American debate in the 1780s and Europe's non-debate in the 2000s is no longer a historical curiosity. It *matters*—urgently. So how are we to account for it? A frequent answer is that it would have been absurd to expect anything else: that, since the present-day European Union is not a state like India in the 1940s, or a would-be state like America in the 1780s, talk of a European constitution would have been misplaced, and an American- or Indian-style constitutional debate redundant.

But that answer is spurious. The European Union may not be a state, but it is unquestionably a polity. It is governed according to elaborate rules, set out in binding treaties, which have the force of law in its member states. These rules have changed a great deal in the fifty years since the Rome Treaty; and it is about as certain as any political prediction can be that, if the Union survives, there will be more changes in the next fifty. The interminable process that led from the decision to draw up a Constitutional Treaty to the ratification of the Lisbon Treaty provided an ideal opportunity for a continent-wide conversation about the possible constitutional futures of the new Europe created by the collapse of Communism and the inclusion of a swath of former Soviet satellites in a union committed to democracy and human rights.

The true answer to my question lies deeper: the theory that integration would spread ineluctably, like an inkblot, from one policy domain to another, had no place for public debate. The end was political, but the means were economic; and the means gradually eclipsed the end. Integration was supposed to spread, irresistibly and irrevocably, from one economic field to another; there would be no breaks in the process, when popular consent would have to be mobilized. Economic success, facts on the ground—market freedom, economies of scale, rapid growth, rising living standards—would be enough to embed the project in the public culture. There was no need to buttress legitimacy of the fact with the legitimacy of shared purposes. That would take care of itself.

Not only was the inkblot theory economistic by definition, but it was also technocratic by definition. As I suggested in chapter 2, those who held it shrank from the crudity and messiness of public politics, which they saw as irrelevant at best and as a threat at worst. That mood is still alive and well in the Brussels village. Economistic technocrats are often skilled at corridor politics, but they shy away from the politics of the stump, the debating chamber, the pamphlet, or the television studio. If they didn't, they would not be technocrats.

Nor would they fit the job description implied by Monnet's subtle blend of pragmatism and idealism. Full-blown federations characteristically start with the "high politics" of foreign policy, defense, and (not least) money. Only later do they extend into the "low politics" of infrastructure development, sectoral intervention, and the like. (The American federal government did not do so on a significant scale until the New Deal.) But, as we saw in chapter 2, the essence of Monnet's scheme was to do the opposite. The "low politics" of economic integration came first; "high politics" would follow later, in God's or Mammon's good time. The Coal and Steel Community started with "low" political sectoral intervention. The successor European Economic Community had a wider remit, but, as befitted its name, it too focused overwhelmingly on economic "low politics": on agriculture, interstate commerce, regional aids, the removal of barriers to free competition, and the creation of an elaborate regulatory framework to harmonize standards. Both left "high politics" to the member states.

"Low politics" were themselves political, of course. Deals had to be brokered; trade-offs had to be agreed; losers had to be compensated. Indeed, the whole European project embodied a trade-off: German respectability in exchange for French-led supranationalism; agricultural protection in exchange for industrial free trade. But the politics involved were quintessentially corridor politics—the sort of politics that technocrats are good at; the sort that, in complex modern societies, need technocratic skills and casts of mind. Not surprisingly, the Brussels Commission has attracted technocrats as jam pots attract wasps. The corridors of its Berlaymont Building resound to the tramp of technocratic feet—belonging to national officials and national lobbyists of all kinds, as well as to EU functionaries. Though the most successful commissioners have usually had political backgrounds, they have generally been technocratic, corridor politicians first and public politicians second.

The classic case is Jean Monnet himself. He was first and foremost a visionary, endowed with a quiet but compelling charisma and an extraordinary capacity to make inspiring leaps of imagination. But he was also a consummate corridor politician who was never elected to any public office. There are plenty of recent examples as well. The most outstanding is Jacques Delors, the most successful Commission president of recent times. Before joining the Commission, he had been a minister under the socialist president François Mitterrand, but he had started his career as an official in the Banque de France and later in the State Planning Commission.

In the same mold was the British commissioner Lord Cockfield (pronounced Co'field), the chief author of the plan for completing the single market in the 1980s, the precursor of monetary union a decade later. Cockfield had served briefly as a Conservative cabinet minister under Margaret Thatcher, but he had started his career in the Inland Revenue and had then become finance director of Boots, Britain's leading pharmacy chain. Like Monnet, he had never been elected to public office. A contrasting case is Roy Jenkins, the first (and so far the only) British Commission president. Jenkins was a "high" politician through and through, enamored of what he liked to call the "grandes lignes" of policy. He had been a highly successful chancellor of the exchequer and home secretary in Britain. In Brussels he was visibly ill at ease: an urbanely rounded peg in a spiky hole.[3]

Today "low politics" are not enough. There will always be a place for them. There are plenty of "low politics" in the member states—indeed in all states, not least the United States. Skilled technocrats will always be in demand, in the Union's institutions as well in national administrations. However, the days when the European project could stay out of high politics are over. One reason is that monetary union—the last great achievement of the technocrats' Europe—burst the banks between low politics and high politics. That is the inner meaning of the 2010 Greek sovereign debt crisis, the harsh austerity measures imposed as concomitants of a bailout, the gyrations in the markets for European bonds, the looming shadow of Greek-style crises in Portugal, Ireland, and Spain, the creation of a €750 billion Eurozone stabilization facility, and, not least, growing German impatience with the role of Europe's paymaster. Since the spring of 2010, the Eurozone has been in turmoil; and since the Eurozone is Europe's heartland, that means that non-Eurozone member states cannot insulate themselves from its troubles.

But though the crisis is financial and economic in form, it is political in substance and origin. The choices it raises go to the heart of European politics. One possible solution would be the secession of the Eurozone's weaker economies. That would mean a two-tier Europe, divided between a rich and competitive core and an uncompetitive, inflation-prone periphery—making nonsense of the commitment to solidarity that is supposed to lie at the heart of the European project. Another possibility is more Greek-style crises and more deflationary austerity packages, imposed by EU authorities and/or the IMF, impoverishing the weaker economies and perhaps destabilizing their governments. A third is to end, or at least mitigate, the mismatch between monetary union and fiscal disunion by giving fiscal powers of some kind to a Eurozone political authority. At the moment of writing, no one can tell how the story will continue, let alone how it will end. But this much is clear. A failure of political imagination and will was responsible for the fatal combination of

monetary union and fiscal disunion. Only a political decision can correct it. We are witnessing the revenge of politics
over economism.

The economic crisis itself, like its predecessor in the
1930s, is political, not technical. The speculative bubble
that procured it was the proximate cause, but the bubble itself—and the regulatory regime and economic policies that
pumped air into the bubble—were the products of deliberate
political choices. Also like the crisis of the 1930s, it has created opportunities for new departures, based on competing
political doctrines as well as on different economic philos-
ophies. No matter how the competition ends, the eventual
outcome will also be the product of political choices, enabled
by political wills. In the United States, the elected president
can help to generate and focus such a will, as Franklin Roo-
sevelt did in the 1930s, and as Obama would like to do now.
But there is no European will and no European political authority to generate one.

The same will almost certainly be true of climate change.
Europe can fairly claim to have done more to combat climate change than the United States, Russia, China, or India.
But at the 2009 climate change conference, that claim cut
no ice. Europe could point to significant achievements and
good intentions, but it had no political leverage. When push
came to shove, the other great economic blocs could and did
ignore it.

The effects of climate change and its impact on global
politics are unlikely to remain as mild as they have been so
far. Here, above all, business as usual is unfeasible. The world's
economic blocs will have to find painful answers to urgent
problems; and the allocation of the pain will be a supremely
high-political matter. It will raise profound questions of dis-
tributive justice, of the obligations that the present genera-

tion owes to future ones, of the proper balance between the claims of poor and rich nations, and of the proper relationship between the human and other species. Such questions are far beyond the scope of low-political technical rationality. To be sure, they also go far beyond the European Union. They are quintessentially global in character, and the answers will have to be global too. But for the Union's leaders to opt out of the global search for answers would be a betrayal of their citizens. And they will be unable to opt in if they cannot speak with one voice and lack the democratic legitimacy to carry their peoples with them.

In one of his most powerful interventions in the American debate of the 1780s, Alexander Hamilton excoriated the "tedious delays—continued negotiation and intrigue—contemptible compromises of the public good" that flowed from the Articles of Confederation that he and his federalist allies were fighting to replace.[4] That is not an exact description of today's European Pushmi-Pullyu. But it is too close to the bone for comfort.

So why the Union's "low" political bias? How should it be overcome? It is, of course, a legacy of the economism of its early days. Less obviously, it is also a child of the cold war, when western Europe could shelter behind America's protective skirts. In those days, the then Community had no reason—and little opportunity—to move into the "high" political sphere. NATO, "high"-political by definition, took care of Europe's security needs; Washington, the new Rome of the "West," was the arena where Europeans did the high politics that really mattered to them. However, Europe is no longer the cockpit of a worldwide contest between an American-led "West" and a Soviet-led "East," and America is no longer the Europeans' guardian and lodestar. In this new world,

Europeans will sooner or later have to find an answer to Kissinger's question, as Americans found an answer to Hamilton's taunts in the 1780s. They can't find an answer without a step change comparable to the one that took place in North America 220 years ago.

The authors of the U.S. Constitution sought, as they put it in immortal phrase, to build "a more perfect union" because bitter experience had taught them that, to survive in a hard world, the liberty they prized had to be rooted in strong and legitimate rule. In this, the Europe of today is closer to the America of the 1780s than most Europeans and Americans realize. After all, Europe's leaders launched the constitutional and Lisbon treaties in the first place because they sensed that the existing architecture of Union governance needed overhaul.

The tragedy is that, unlike the authors of the U.S. Constitution, they were both too modest and too arrogant. They lacked the vaulting political ambition of the American federalists; and they did not involve the union's citizen body in their project. But it would be a counsel of despair to assume that twenty-first-century Europeans are, for some reason, incapable of holding a European equivalent of the national conversation that made the American step change possible. We may fail to do so, but we owe it to ourselves to try.

What should a European conversation be about? How should it be conducted? The first essential is to jump over the tramlines of the academic discipline of international relations. For the self-styled "realists" who largely populate that discipline, the nation-state, conceived of as an impermeable billiard ball, is the key actor in international affairs.[5] Philosophical, moral, and ideological questions are irrelevant and ought to be excluded from serious debate. States are rational political actors, first cousins to the rational economic actor whom the current economic crisis brought down in flames. They pursue their rationally determined interests as rational economic actors pursue theirs. They may disguise their pursuit with high-flown, moralistic, or ideological verbiage. But the verbiage is camouflage; strip it away and the clear, hard bones of interest invariably come into view. Just as many mainstream modern economists have forgotten the philosophical and moral concerns of the founders of classical "political economy," such as Adam Smith, Thomas Malthus, and David Ricardo, many international relations specialists have turned their backs on the normative sea in which ministers, officials, and opinion makers invariably swim—even if they are not conscious of doing so.

In the Anglophone world, where "realism" permeates the public culture, the result is a thin, two-dimensional, and above all, banal approach to the past, present, and possible futures of the European project. For the European Union is not, and never has been, a mere group of self-interested states. Realpolitik helped to launch the European project, but realpolitik alone cannot explain its genesis or its astonishing early successes. Both were rooted in a shared belief that the catastrophes of the two world wars had stemmed from moral as well as political failures, and that to repair the damage an ethic of mutual understanding and forgiveness had to outweigh national interests, narrowly conceived. That was what Monnet meant when he said his aim was to "unite men," not to "coalesce states." Monnet's dream has faded, but it has not vanished from the European scene. The Union is composed of states, of course; and the states pursue what their leaders take to be their interests. But it also constrains the states concerned, as I argued in the previous chapter, and the constraints stem from a complex process of mutual learning—

moral and philosophical as well as practical—that social scientific "realism" cannot capture.

Equally, a focus on the institutional nuts and bolts beloved of specialists in European studies confuses more than it illuminates. Structure is a function of purpose; interests are defined by ideas and, ultimately, by the moral assumptions they encapsulate. A frequent theme of academic discourse about European politics is a supposed contrast between something called "rhetoric" and something else called "reality."[6] But rhetoric is an aspect of reality, while reality is structured by rhetoric. If rhetoric is defined as persuasive utterance, as it should be, then realists who rubbish opinions they dislike as rhetoric are themselves using a rather fly-blown rhetorical trope. A worthwhile debate on Europe after Lisbon would have to dig much deeper than tropes of this sort. It would have to grapple with fundamental philosophical and ethical questions from which the present generation of European leaders, aided and abetted by all too many commentators and academics, shy away—questions about the nature of politics and political man and woman, the possibilities of political action, the meaning of democracy in the postmodern world of the twenty-first century, the nature of European civilization and the European ideal, and the place Europeans should seek to occupy in the world we now live in.

This, above all, is what the constitutional debates of late eighteenth-century America have to teach the Europe of the early twenty-first. The American debaters were practical men, not study-bound theorists. They were no strangers to the politics of interest: slave states against free states, big states against small ones. But they did not deal in interest alone. The tumult of revolution and war had swept them from their old political and intellectual moorings. They had freed themselves from the British Crown—almost certainly against their original intentions—and they had to decide what to do with their freedom and how to safeguard it. In doing so, they pillaged the learning of the past and drew on the scholarship of their own time. But with astonishing practical and intellectual creativity, they also broke through the barriers of the conventional wisdom of the day and hammered out a new political science suited to their needs. Today's Europeans cannot follow slavishly where they led, but we need at least a dash of their willingness to think from first principles.

The beginning of wisdom is to acknowledge that, despite the Lisbon Treaty, the European project is still mired in a shaming paradox. The Union has been an astonishingly successful agent of democratization, perhaps the most successful in democracy's long and contested history. With all its undoubted shortcomings and dangers, the incorporation of ten former Communist countries in East Central Europe, some of them strangers to democracy even before they were absorbed into the Soviet empire, has dramatically widened the scope of democratic self-government and the rule of law, just as the incorporation of Portugal, Spain, and Greece did in the early 1980s.

The change has come so quickly and so peacefully that it is easy to assume that it was foreordained. Nothing could be further from the truth. Twenty years ago, the former Soviet satellites of East Central Europe had only just emerged from the Communist straitjacket to discover that their countries were bankrupt, their economies grotesquely inefficient, their living standards far below those of the West, and their civil societies deformed.

We know now that the region did not lurch into a new form of authoritarianism, but no one knew that in 1990. It would be rash to assume that democracy, in any of its manifold senses, is safely entrenched throughout the European continent even now. As earlier chapters showed, ugly forces threaten it, most obviously in the ex-Communist new member states, but also in west European countries such as Denmark, France, Belgium, the Netherlands, Italy, and the United Kingdom. Yet despite such threats, democratic institutions, backed by guaranteed human rights, are in place throughout the vast swath of territory that now comprises the European Union. And for that extraordinary achievement, the Union deserves the lion's share of the credit.

Yet a scandal lurks behind the arras. The constitution of the Union itself violates the democratic principles it has helped to implant in most of its new member states and many of its old ones. At its heart lies a much-discussed but ill-understood "democratic deficit," which is also a deficit of leadership, will, and legitimacy—and ultimately of politics as such. Its institutions cannot mobilize consent because they are not rooted in consent; because they can't mobilize consent, they can't lead the Union into the high-political sphere and overcome the threat of global irrelevance.

With lapidary economy, the Union's motto, United in Diversity, encapsulates the vision that inspired Monnet and the other founders, and that still animates the better angels of Europe's leaders. But it implies a tension—an inescapable and healthy tension, to be sure—between the general interest of the Union as a whole and the particular interests of the member states. There is nothing wrong or strange in that. The same is true of all federal and confederal systems—indeed of multilevel governance as such. Europe's tragedy is that the Union's institutions lack the moral authority to pursue the general interest wholeheartedly and effectively:

that the legitimacy of the fact is no longer enough. The result is that the parts speak too loudly and the whole too softly.

However, this is dangerous territory. One of the curiosities of what academics pompously call "the literature" is a bland insistence that the democratic deficit does not exist, and (somewhat incongruously) that insofar as it does exist, it is a good thing. EU governance, says the Harvard political scientist Andrew Moravcsik, is as democratic as the governance of its member states—and, for that matter, of all real-world advanced democracies. To ask for more democracy at EU level is to ask for the impossible, indeed for the undesirable. It is a form of utopianism that has no place in serious social-scientific analysis.[7] In similar vein, Mark Leonard argues that critics of the democratic deficit miss the point of the European Union. It is a "network," not an embryo federation; and it neither can nor should mimic the constitutional arrangements of democratic states.[8] At bottom, Moravcsik and Leonard are saying the same thing—Moravcsik with impressive scholarship and Leonard with engaging *brio.* The European Union is what it is. It can never be anything else, and it should not try.

For their part, critics of the democratic deficit interpret the term in a wide variety of sometimes incompatible ways. When the notion first surfaced in the late 1970s, it had a precise but limited meaning. So long as the decisions of the Community's Council of Ministers had to be unanimous, the argument went, all the governments represented in it must, by definition, have agreed to all its decisions. That meant that they were all accountable for all Community decisions to their electorates, or to their democratically elected parliaments. Community democracy was an emanation of national democracy. But when majority voting replaced national vetoes, that would no longer be true. The government of a sovereign nation-state might be outvoted; the will of the sovereign people of that state might be flouted.

It would no longer be possible to hold all member governments to account for all decisions, and because they could not all be held to account, none of them could be. National governments would no longer be a channel through which democratic legitimacy flowed from the national to the Community level.[9] The decision to make the European Parliament directly elected, and a long line of subsequent decisions to give it more say in the Union's legislative process, followed from that analysis. But, as I shall try to show in a moment, it is hard to argue that the constitution of the EU as a whole, as distinct from the constitutions of its member states, now conforms to democratic norms.

Today two very different interpretations of the democratic deficit are in contention. The first underpinned a contorted ruling of the German Constitutional Court on the Lisbon Treaty in the summer of 2009. A cross-party group from the far right and far left had sought to block the Lisbon Treaty by taking a case to the Constitutional Court, arguing that the treaty contravened Germany's Basic Law—in other words, the German constitution. The court found against the complainants and ruled that the treaty was compatible with the Basic Law. This made it possible for Germany to ratify the treaty, and she duly did so.

But, though Lisbon passed the court's test of constitutionality, the judgment was hedged about with ominous caveats. Two stand out. First, the court declared that there was "no uniform European people" capable of expressing "its majority will." Secondly, it held that elections to the European Parliament did not "take due account of equality," in other words, that some voters were represented more generously than others. (What this really meant was that small countries were overrepresented and big ones—notably Germany—underrepresented.) The net effect was what the court termed a "structural democratic deficit." So long as the EU remained a union of sovereign states, in which the peoples of the states were the sole source of political authority, the democratic deficit would continue. Yet, with a bizarre twist, the court also held that it was precisely because the EU was and would remain nothing more than a union of states that the treaty did not infringe German sovereignty and that the German government was free to ratify it. The message was clear: "thus far, but no further." German democracy ruled out—and would forever rule out—EU democracy.

Now this is a highly eccentric interpretation of the democratic deficit, stemming from a particular (not to say peculiar) conception of democracy. On the Constitutional Court's assumptions, the United States, where all states, irrespective of population, are equally represented in the Senate, and where the Electoral College votes that determine who wins the presidency do not necessarily coincide with the popular vote, is not a democracy. In the days when Scotland and Wales had more seats in the Westminster Parliament than their populations warranted, and Northern Ireland fewer, the United Kingdom was not a democracy. Since its First-Past-the-Post electoral system still produces wild disparities between votes cast and parliamentary seats won, it may not be a democracy even now. On the court's assumptions, even Germany is not truly democratic: parties with less than 5 percent of the popular vote are debarred from representation in the Bundestag, so the people who voted for them are disfranchised.

As for the court's assumption that there can be no democracy without a "uniform people," that runs counter to past experience in the world's two largest democracies, India and the United States. Was there really a "uniform people" in India immediately after independence? Was there one in the United States in the early years of the American Republic—or for that matter in the period after the devastation and bloodshed of the Civil War? It seems unlikely.

The British Raj in India rested ultimately on force, but whenever possible it was kept in the background. The central theme of British policy was a strategy of divide and rule. It was bound to be: some twelve hundred British administrators could not possibly have governed a huge subcontinent without the cooperation of local elites, and all too often cooperation was earned by pitting one elite against another. Brahmins were taken at their own valuation as the highest caste in the complex Hindu hierarchy. So-called martial races—the Sikhs were supposedly the most martial—were favored over the allegedly effete, notably the Bengalis. The last thing the British wanted was to hammer the huge variety of Indian castes, religions, language groups, economic interests, and status hierarchies into a united whole on the pattern of a European state. On the contrary, they did their best to pickle them in historicist brine. In some respects, they did unify the subcontinent; the elaborate Indian railway network was an example. But, for most of the time, as Maria Misra nicely puts it, most of them saw India "as a living museum of traditions, to be categorized, ranked and preserved at all costs."[10] And according to her, many of the traditions concerned were ersatz inventions of the British and their Indian collaborators, not legacies of an ageless past.

Some more-or-less democratic elements were grafted on to the Raj in the 1930s, but they were very feeble; and, in any case, they too were intended to preserve divisions at least as much as to bridge them. So far from creating a uniform people, the British manipulated the subcontinent's divisions of geography, religion, caste, and language for their own advantage and helped to fortify them in doing so. Besides, large tracts of what became Indian territory belonged to a huge variety of princely states, comprising around a third of the subcontinent's land mass and around a fifth of its total population. The princely states were controlled ultimately by the British, but their structures differed widely, and they enjoyed differing degrees of internal autonomy. Of course, elements of a common culture cut across India's divisions, but that is equally true of modern Europe. In any case, commonality does not entail uniformity.

Insofar as the Indians are now a "uniform people"—and "uniform" is not the word that springs most readily to the lips—it is because India became a democracy *before* anything that could be called a uniform people had come into existence: because the Indian elite took a gamble on popular government, despite the mass poverty, widespread illiteracy, caste divisions, and linguistic and cultural differences of their fragile new nation. The Indian demos was made by democracy, not democracy by the demos.[11] Here too Misra puts it well. Today, she writes, there is an "overarching sense of Indianness," but the arch is built on the discovery that democracy provides "a relatively peaceful way of brokering . . . competing claims."[12] The whole process is a perfect illustration of a gnomic phrase of the celebrated German philosopher Jürgen

Habermas: "Peoples emerge only with the constitutions of their states."[13]

Much the same is true of the United States. There was no "uniform people" in the thinly settled, poorly developed former British colonies, strung out along the Atlantic seaboard and largely populated by subsistence farmers, in the decades following the American Revolution. Socially and culturally, the gifted and imaginative political elite that crafted the federal Constitution was far from representative of the people for whom it spoke. (And, of course, the last thing it wanted was an American democracy.) But despite the hopes of the founders, a democracy of sorts, confined to adult white males, gradually inserted itself into the political system. The American demos was forged in the passionate, sometimes tumultuous, public debates that followed.[14]

But even then, there was no "uniform" American people. Native Americans and black slaves were excluded from the political nation. As late as 1958–59, when I first visited the United States, segregation was still in force in the Deep South, effectively disfranchising the black population, as well as subjecting it to indignity and humiliation. Yet most Americans thought of their country as a democracy, and most of America's allies elsewhere in the "West" did so too.

There are comparable examples nearer home—not least in Germany itself. Is the Turkish minority in Germany really part of a uniform German people? Do the Muslim minorities in France, Denmark, the Netherlands, and Britain belong to "uniform" French, Danish, Butch, and British peoples? Hardly. As the previous chapter tried to show, the truth is that, in European country after European country, uniformity is giving way to pluralism, as premodern ethnic communities find their place in the postmodern sun, while newer ethnic and religious minorities, composed of or descended from immigrants from what used to be called the Third World, struggle for recognition. In this Europe (indeed, in this world), the notion of a uniform people, and of a democracy founded on such a people, is profoundly dangerous, as well as untrue to the facts.

Peeping out furtively from behind the German Constitutional Court's judgment is a notion of tribal democracy, faintly but alarmingly reminiscent of East Central Europe's bloody past. "We must love one another or die," wrote W. H. Auden. That was asking too much. But we do have to learn to live with one another; and living with one another means accepting difference, rejoicing in difference, and negotiating differences. That is the inner meaning of the Good Friday agreement in Northern Ireland, of asymmetric devolution in Spain, of the emergence of a federal Belgium, of the secession of Slovakia from what used to be Czechoslovakia, and of the still-timid reemergence of ancient provinces in hitherto centralized France. Slowly, sometimes reluctantly and even painfully, Europeans are beginning to come to terms with difference, to accept its inevitability and legitimacy, and to bridge differences that once seemed unbridgeable. Supplementing Monnet's dream is a vision of a Europe that recognizes and reconciles its peoples, as they really are, in all their marvelous complexity.

That does not dispose of the democratic deficit, however. The second interpretation is less precise than the German Constitutional Court's, but more in keeping with European politics as they are practiced in the twenty-first century and on a deeper (and far more important) level with the culture of democracy as it has developed in the millennia since Pericles. In this second interpretation, the deficit is one of comprehension, representation, and accountability. The three are linked. You can't hold institutions you don't understand to account; and it is hard to see how they can represent you. And no one outside a tiny group of Euro-actors and Euro-academics understands how the European Union works.

National politics often baffle ordinary citizens, not least because national governments are entangled in increasingly complex webs of European and global interdependence. But the citizens of the Union's member states mostly have at least a vague notion of what national political parties stand for, and who national leaders and would-be leaders are. In the time-honored phrase, they can, if they wish, "throw the rascals out." And there is, at least, a tenuous connection between their votes and the policies their governments pursue,

None of this is true of Union politics. Voters in European elections can't throw the rascals out. The connection between their votes and Union policies is not just tenuous but invisible. There is no shortage of rascals, but the most egregious of them belong to national governments and administrations, not to European institutions of any kind. Even the ones that do belong to European bodies—notably, Commission and Council permanent officials—are mostly out of reach of European voters and their representatives in the European Parliament. Worse still, there are no Europe-wide political parties to focus debate and offer choices to a European electorate. European citizens vote in European elections when they do (and, as earlier chapters have shown, increasing numbers don't) to punish or reward *national* political parties, fighting on essentially national platforms. And though the European Parliament's role in the Union's legislative process has grown immeasurably in recent years, the process itself is both labyrinthine and impenetrable by outsiders.

In any case, the right to propose legislation still rests with the unelected Commission, while the Parliament's powers over Union legislation are matched by those of the Council of Ministers, which represents *national* governments and administrations, ultimately responsible to *national* electorates. It is the European Council, not the Council of Ministers, that lays down the broad lines of EU policy, and the European Council consists of the heads of member state governments. Herman Van Rompuy, now president of the Council, and Baroness Ashton, the Union's first "high representative" for foreign affairs, were appointed by the member governments, in an arcane process of backstairs horse trading, punctuated by unattributable briefing and leaks. Union citizens did not get a look in.

Here, however, a stumbling block comes into the story. By definition, it makes no sense to talk of a democratic deficit without first talking of democracy. But talking of democracy is not as easy as one might think. There is no single, monolithic, universally accepted interpretation of that soul-stirring, world-conquering word. (The greatest single error of the Bush administration's policies toward Iraq was to imagine that there is, or can be.) Democracy is plural, not singular; and it is a culture as well as a set of institutions. The current Russian regime insists that theirs is a "sovereign democracy"; Iranian ayatollahs speak of "Islamic democracy." The Soviet satellites in East Central Europe claimed to be "people's democracies"; Singapore's effectively one-party state has been dubbed a "social democracy." For Abraham Lincoln, democracy meant "government of the people, by the people, for the people." For the British High Tory L. S. Amery, it meant "government of the people, for the people, with but not by the people."[15]

Since the term first appeared on the scene in ancient Athens, its meaning has changed repeatedly, and so has its reputation. The famous quote from Pericles that I used as one of the epigraphs of this chapter was not a piece of dispassionate social science, such as might be offered to a peer-reviewed journal. (Not that many social scientists are as dispassionate as they pretend.) Like Lincoln at Gettysburg, his closest modern counterpart, Pericles was a political leader, engaged in hard-fought political battles, seeking to mobilize support for his person and his vision of the future. By no means all of his fellow citizens agreed with him; some of them thought his vision profoundly dangerous and even corrupting.

Plato, as famous a son of Athens as Pericles himself, wrote one of the most passionate and resonant works of political philosophy ever penned to prove, among other things, that the form of government that Pericles extolled was unjust, immoral, and contrary to the natural order. Plato's equally famous pupil, Aristotle, was less savage than Plato but almost as critical. As the British political theorist John Dunn aptly puts it, democracy, for Aristotle, was a "regime of naked group interest, unapologetically devoted to serving the many at the expense of the wealthier, the better, the more elevated, the more fastidious or virtuous."[16] For more than two thousand years, the best minds of Europe gave far more credence to the legacy of Plato and Aristotle than to that of Pericles.

The legacy of the Roman Republic was at least as influential. The Republic was not a democracy. Power was shared between the Senate, dominated by often ancient aristocratic clans and the People, through an inordinately complex system of checks and balances. In early-modern Europe, a dazzling array of political thinkers and leaders sought to distill the lessons of its history. Certain widely held conclusions emerged from these musings. The first was that republican liberty—the liberty that the Roman Republic had cherished and for centuries preserved—was a precondition of human well-being and a source of civic glory and greatness. The second was that liberty of that sort depended on civic virtue; and that, so far from being innate, such virtue depended on republican institutions that combined monarchical, aristocratic, and democratic features, so as to constrain both the selfish ambitions of the patricians and the equally selfish passions of the plebs.

The third lesson was harder. It was that unconstrained popular government—the kind of government found in ancient Athens—would sooner or later degenerate into a kind of mob rule and founder in a sea of strife and chaos. The end result would be tyranny and the snuffing out of liberty. The collapse of originally vital (though highly unstable) popular governments, established in many Italian city-states in the eleventh and twelfth centuries, seemed to bear out that prognosis.[17] So, much more tragically, did the story of the French Revolution and its fearsome progress from plebeian frenzy, to blood-soaked terror, to Napoleon's dictatorship at home and aggression abroad.

At first sight, the connection between today's EU and the ancient world, or even Renaissance Italy or revolutionary France, is slight to the point of invisibility. The democracy that arrived in northwestern Europe in the second half of the nineteenth century and the first quarter of the twentieth, that Germany and Italy embraced after World War II, and that conquered the former Soviet satellites after 1989, has virtually nothing in common with the *demokratia* of Periclean Athens or the participative self-government of the Italian city-states. We call it "representative democracy"—sometimes with a sigh of regret for the lost glories of antiquity. The people do not govern themselves directly. However, ultimate sovereignty lies with them, and they do choose those who govern them. Government—rule—is rooted in the consent of the governed.

So defined, democracy has had many interpreters, some friendly and some hostile; and in any case, it has taken a variety of forms. That said, the interpretation offered by the great Austrian-born, Harvard-based political economist Joseph Schumpeter has been particularly persuasive. With exhilarating brutality, Schumpeter dismissed what he called the "classical" theory of democracy as nostalgic and dangerous humbug. In truth, the democratic process was a kind of market, where teams of politicians competed for votes, in the way that business firms compete for custom. The ordinary citizen's only role was to decide which team was to govern her. Except in "small and primitive societies,"[18] the notion that she and her fellow citizens could govern themselves was a nostalgic and dangerous absurdity. Outside the ranks of professional social scientists, Schumpeter had few avowed followers. (There were plenty of unavowed ones.) Yet his teachings distilled—and at the same time reinforced—two essential features of the dominant understanding of democracy in present-day Europe: an understanding I shall call liberal-individualist.

It is liberal in that its central value is freedom of choice; it is individualist in that it ignores the manifold social and collective elements in the rich and varied liberal tradition, and sees the individual citizen as an island unto herself, making her choices in the privacy of her own soul. For liberal individualists it is up to her, and only to her, to decide what her interests are. That *individual* decision determines how she votes. She rewards political leaders who seem likely to govern her in accordance with her view of her interests, and punishes those who do not. She goes to the political marketplace equipped with her self-chosen, predetermined interests, like a knowing customer entering a grocery store, equipped with a predetermined shopping list. At the moment of choice, she is a solipsist.

But the Schumpeterian individual is an odd creature. In real life, atomistic individuals, solitary captains of their own souls, like the driven Captain Ahab in Melville's *Moby Dick*, are so rare that we have a special label for them: "autistic." The vast majority of us are linked to others by ties of kinship, education, ethnicity, religion, locality, and occupation, to mention only a few; these ties make us who we are, and we could not cut loose from them in the polling station, even if we wished to. Most liberal individualists know this, but they ignore it. The liberal-individualist understanding of democracy is uncomfortable with groups, group loyalties, and group interests. Everyone knows that they exist—but as blemishes, pimples on democracy's nether parts. They are "special interests," intrinsically illegitimate and potentially dangerous. They distort the political marketplace, in the way that monopolistic rent seekers distort the economic one.

A classic example is the liberal-individualist uneasiness about class. Classes, class interests, and class loyalties patently exist. Though their ties have weakened in the advanced postindustrial societies of today, they still affect the way large numbers of people vote. But, unlike social liberals in the tradition of the British L. T. Hobhouse and the American John Dewey, liberal-individualist commentators wish they didn't: the appearance of "Joe six-pack" in the Democratic primaries in 2008 was widely seen as a regrettable regression to the past. The same applies (nowadays even more strongly) to ethnicity. The fact that black Americans were disproportionately for Obama in 2008 was seen, in some quarters, as a strike against him. In the United Kingdom, even some opponents of the Iraq War were shocked to learn that many Muslim voters switched from Tony Blair's Labour Party to the antiwar Liberal Democrats because they saw the war as an assault on Islam. In the liberal-individualist understanding of democracy, workers, farmers, Muslims, Jews, Catholics, Irish people, Bretons, Corsicans, and the like should dump their group identities and loyalties outside the door of the polling station. The fact that they don't and can't is seen as a dirty little secret, not to be mentioned in polite society.

The implications of these embarrassments and discomfitures go very deep. As I tried to show in the previous chapter, the politics of recognition is *about* groups—about conflicting group identities and claims, and about the negotiation and resolution of such conflicts. In reality, the dirty little secret is no secret. We all know that groups exist, that there are conflicts between them, that group differences are often negotiated, and that some conflicts are even resolved. But because the prevailing liberal-individualist understanding has no place for collectivities, Europeans have no language in which to talk about these processes and no narrative to explain them. The moral panic over multiculturalism I mentioned in the previous chapter is only one of many consequences.

For Schumpeter, political leaders were professionals who had to be allowed to get on with the job of government as they saw fit, without interference from the voters. Citizens decided what their interests were in the privacy of their own hearts and then voted accordingly; that was the alpha and omega of their role in the democratic process. What Schumpeter excoriated as "back-seat driving" by an ignorant and irrational public was inimical to democracy; once they had voted, the people were supposed to keep quiet and leave ruling to their chosen rulers. The American Civil War, he thought, was a terrible warning of what might happen if ordinary voters got too excited about politics.[19]

Few contemporary liberal individualists would put it as crudely as that, but here too, Schumpeter's brutal reductionism illuminates a crucial element in the liberal-individualist narrative. Since interests are individually determined and individually translated into votes, there is no place in the democratic process for public reasoning or debate. Political leaders try to persuade voters to vote for them, of course, but in the way that business firms hawk their wares to potential consumers. Communication is a one-way street, from would-be sellers, advised by spin doctors, campaign managers, and opinion pollsters, to possible buyers. There is no room for dialogue, either between voters and politicians or between voters and voters. The striking absence of pan-European debate over the Constitutional and Lisbon treaties was part of a syndrome of silence.

The prevailing, liberal-individualist understanding is not the only one, however. Fragments of much older ideas, left over from earlier periods, float in the European air, like leaves in an autumn wind. Alongside the liberal-individualist understanding of democracy run traces of a weaker, but still persistent, republican understanding. In practice, the two are not polar opposites. There are elements of both in most democratic systems. Real-world republicans are usually tinged with liberal individualism; there is a smidgeon of republicanism in many liberal individualists. And the two overlap on one crucial point: liberty is a core value for both. For all that, there are profound differences between them. For republicans, liberty means more than free choice. It means the "Roman liberty" I mentioned a moment ago: freedom from domination. A slave with a kind, tolerant, permissive master is still a slave. She may enjoy plenty of freedom of choice in practice, but she does so only at her master's pleasure.[20] And slavery degrades the master as well as the slave.

More importantly, the two picture the democratic process in different ways. For liberal individualists, the central characters in the democratic story are the freely choosing individual and the political entrepreneurs for whom she votes or refuses to vote. For republicans, there is a third term in the equation: a public realm, where civic virtue is learned and practiced, where the citizens of a political community make collective choices about their common identity and preferred destiny and try together to master fate. It is a realm, not just of head counting, but of public reasoning. Democratic citizens are not islands unto themselves. They do not determine their preferences in autistic isolation. Their preferences emerge from a process of deliberation, contestation, and mutual discovery, through which they become better citizens—and better people.

During the English civil wars of the seventeenth century, John Milton, passionate republican as well as majestic poet, eulogized then revolutionary London as the "mansion house of liberty," effervescent with "disputing, reasoning, reading, inventing, discoursing" that fortified the "gallant bravery" of those engaged in them.[21] That note has recurred again and again in the long history of republican rhetoric—from the racy, epigrammatic prose of Tom Paine during the American Revolution to Abraham Lincoln's Gettysburg Address to the gripping oratory of the great French socialist leader Jean Jaurès.

Against this background, the European Union's current travails acquire a sharper outline. Clearly, Union governance violates the norms of both understandings of democracy. For the liberal-individualist understanding to function, citizens must know, in the time-honored phrase, "where the buck stops": who is responsible for the decisions that they like or dislike. Otherwise, they can't know whom to reward or punish with their votes. But the EU has no buck—or, at least, no buck that stops. There is only an endless maze of indeterminacy. To be sure, this is increasingly true of the member states as well: there is merit in Moravcsik's view that national and EU democracy are not as far apart as critics of the latter are apt to assume. But that is only another way of saying that some of the functions that the classical, Westphalian state performed in its great days can now be performed only on the European level and that the global marketplace has taken over others. It would be perverse to argue that, because national governance violates democratic norms, European governance should do so too.

As for the republican understanding, European governance fails the two most important tests that the republican tradition implies: the test of nondomination and the test of a public realm. Though there are plenty of legal safeguards against arbitrary power, the interlocking technocracies and obscure negotiations that largely determine Union policy often *look* arbitrary to Union citizens. Liberty as freedom from domination does not depend solely on laws and regulations, of which the Union has plenty. It also depends on visibility and transparency, in which it is grievously lacking. Above all, there is no European public realm, where collective choices can be hammered out and fate mastered.

In the Union's early days, there were signs that such a realm might emerge as the project bedded down: Monnet's Action Committee for the United States of Europe was, in a way, a step toward one. But the triumph of untamed capitalism in the 1980s and 1990s put paid to hopes of that sort. The very idea that fate could be mastered came to seem fanciful and absurd. Fate—otherwise known as free, competitive markets—was an iron cage from which only backward-looking fools and romantic utopians imagined they could break out. Free-market economics was increasingly seen as a natural science, like physics, with inescapable laws that economists had discovered and that only they fully understood. These laws were givens, beyond dispute. They belonged to the same unchallengeable category as Newton's discovery of gravity or Crick and Watson's of the double helix. These assumptions still govern global capital and foreign exchange markets and linger in the air above the chancelleries and finance ministries of Europe. Even now, despite the crisis of untamed capitalism that devastated the global economy in 2008 and 2009, political leaders are remarkably reluctant to challenge them.

At this point, the great debate over the American Constitution comes back into the story. For Europe at least, the liberal-individualist understanding of democracy is not enough. Europe, even more than the world's other economic blocs, cannot afford to drift onward wherever fate may take it. But the vision of the citizen as an autistic consumer, driven by individual interest, and of the polity as a shopping mall where policy sellers offer their wares to buyers, offers no alternative to drift. The global questions that press in on Europeans—climate change, energy shortages, the desperate poverty of the world's "bottom billion," international terrorism, and above all, the waning of the West and Fareed Zakaria's "rise of the rest"—will have to be answered collectively, through public debate and deliberation as well as by political leaders, if they are to be answered at all. The same applies to the crisis of the Eurozone.

The answers will have to be *European*, not national. The European Union's member states, acting separately, or even by finding the lowest common denominator of agreement between them, lack the leverage to make their answers bite. However wise their leaders and clever their policies, they are bound to be at the mercy of events—the playthings of fate. To ask for European answers is to ask for a European public realm, underpinned and enabled by authoritative European institutions. This implies a vision of Europe as a great republic, highly differentiated, of course, but united enough to hold its own in a cruel and sometimes hostile world. With obvious differences of place, time, and vocabulary, that was the vision that animated the American federalists who founded the United States.

For them, federalism was an urgent necessity, not a theorist's dream. But it was much more than an institutional toolbox, designed to cope with the immediate problems of the day. It sprang from a particular, quintessentially republican conception of the public realm, of civic virtue, of citizenship, of liberty, and of political man. (There were no political women then.) The American federalists sought to secure republican liberty—liberty as self-government by free citizens. Their ideal was not original. It went back to republican theories hammered out in the English civil war, to the city-states of Renaissance Italy, and before that to republican Rome. But, as Samuel Beer has shown in his magisterial study of the making of the United States, they found a highly original solution to a problem that had baffled thinkers and practical politicians for centuries: the problem of size.[22]

It had been assumed that republican liberty could flourish only in small polities. The trouble was that small polities were vulnerable to big predators. The obvious solution was to combine small polities in a league or confederacy; but that solution had just been tried, with disastrous results, in post-Revolutionary America. The Confederation of newly independent former British colonies was weak, fissiparous, and prone to gridlock. The states retained their sovereignty and independence. As a result, the center was too feeble to pursue the common interest, and the individual states were constantly tempted to engage in free riding at the expense of the whole. The federalists' answer was to vest sovereignty in the whole American people and to juxtapose elected state governments with an elected federal government. At the same time, they devised a complex and subtle system of checks and balances to guard against the danger of tyranny by the center over the base, and by majorities over minorities. They combined diversity at the base with unity at the center, and they protected the combination with authoritative institutions strong enough to counter the inevitable arrogance of power.

Europe cannot adopt the American model lock, stock, and barrel, and few Europeans dream of doing so. There have been ugly chapters in American history (as there have in everyone's history), and there is a lot wrong with the practical workings of present-day American federalism. Quite apart from that, the Europe of the twenty-first century and the America of the 1780s are very different places. But, though no one in her right mind would try to transplant American federalism in European soil, the insights of the early American federalists have much to teach a Europe trying to find its place in an unfamiliar and dangerous world. They saw that only a strong government at the center could protect the values they prized, but they recognized the danger of arbitrary power and sought safeguards against it. They realized that the sovereign people could exercise their sovereignty on different levels of government at the same time. And, as they showed when they launched the national conversation that mobilized support for their Constitution, they grasped the need for a public realm of reflection and debate.

The last point is particularly pertinent. For now—though only for now—formal constitution making, of the sort that took place in the American convention in 1787 or the Indian Constituent Assembly after independence, can wait. A federal Europe will need a federal constitution, based on the separation of powers, the protection of human rights, and the principle of subsidiarity I mentioned in chapter 3. It will have to reflect the special needs and peculiarities of an increasingly multicultural and diverse Europe; it cannot be a carbon copy of other federal constitutions. That said, it will probably have more in common with the light-touch, strongly decentralist federalism of Switzerland than with the heavy-handed legalism of the German Federal Republic. But constitution mongering of this sort is not (or not yet) to the point. The task now is to adapt the Union's existing institutions to encourage the emergence of a public realm and the growth of a European demos. The goal is a political Europe. And the way to reach it is through politics.

Two early steps suggest themselves. The European Council has now acquired a president. He is an obscure, gray, almost ostentatiously uncharismatic figure—a technocratic corridor politician *in excelsis*. That was why the heads of government chose him: a public politician might have stolen their thunder. But, in principle at least, a small change in the treaty could perfectly well provide for the direct election of the president by the people of Europe. Candidates would have to explain what they stood for; alternative visions of Europe's future would have to be debated. It would be a gamble, of course. Worthy candidates might not present themselves; the turnout might be low. But unless Europe's elites are willing to gamble on democracy, as India's did after independence, the Union will never escape from its hobbles. The same applies to a second obvious early step: Union-wide referenda on fundamental questions such as the admission of more new members and the still-fudged choice between federalism and confederalism. That too would be a gamble. But that too would help to turn the twenty-seven demoi of the Union's member states into a European demos.

There are three main objections to a European federalism. The first is that Europe is too diverse. There are too many languages, too many histories, too many nationalities, too many cultures for a federal union to bed down. Here, India, rather than America, is the right comparator. In the European Union there are 23 official languages and 60 indigenous regional or minority languages. In India, the world's biggest federation as well as its biggest democracy, the constitution recognizes 22 languages, but there are 350 "major" ones.[23] Indian federalism is not perfect, any more than is American federalism, but it has survived and, on the whole, prospered for more than half a century, despite desperate poverty, gross inequality, and profound religious and cultural divisions. It is hard to see why some iron law should decree that Europeans must be less apt for federalism than Indians.

The second objection—heard mainly in the United Kingdom but also in some of the new member states bristling with a raw, assertive nationalism—is that a federal Europe would be, as Tony Blair used to insist when the European Constitutional Treaty was in the making, a "super-state," crashing through the garden walls of nationhood and reducing the treasured specificities of tradition, identity, and culture to a uniform rubble. Now, by a strange irony, this is exactly what federalists are against. It is what federal unions do *not* do. According to the *Shorter Oxford English Dictionary*, "federal" means, among other things, "of or pertaining to or of the nature of that form of government in which two or more states constitute a political unity, while remaining independent as to their internal affairs." "Federalize" means, first, "to unite in a federal union" and secondly, "to decentralize; to take from the central authority and hand over to the federal bodies in the state or states in a union." Federalism, in other words, is of its essence decentralist, not centralist. It is designed to reconcile diversity wherever possible with union wherever necessary.

The third objection is a child of the heady bubble years of the 1990s and early 2000s, when America's global hegemony seemed impervious and when Europe was preoccupied with the demanding projects of monetary union and enlargement to the east. It contains two parts. In the first place it says that, whatever romantic utopians may imagine, Europe is not moving toward federalism and never will. Federalists should therefore save their breath to cool their porridge. Secondly, it says that Europe's existing constitutional order is already ideally suited to the tasks that the Union needs to perform and will remain so for the foreseeable future. In effect, it posits a future that will be like the present, only more so. In that future there will be no sharp discontinuities or disorientating crises. All is for the best in the best of all possible Europes, and it always will be. Drift is not only inevitable, it is also desirable.

For a while, this new version of Fukyuama's end of history looked quite plausible. Unfortunately, it is now clear that history has not ended after all. At this moment, Europeans are grappling with the effects of a volcanic discontinuity, which has destroyed monetary value across the continent (indeed across the world), on a scale not seen since the Second World War. The full effects are still unknown, but it is already clear that the untaming of capitalism that has dominated global economic history for the last thirty years has not procured a nirvana of ever-growing prosperity, harmony, and contentment; and there is no reason to believe that such a nirvana is waiting beyond the horizon. So far from inaugurating the end of history, the febrile, conflicted world without an "East" or a "West" that is now taking shape is likely to see all too much of it. To help them understand the dynamics of that world, Europeans would do better to turn to Machiavelli and Madison than to Hayek or even Keynes.

To protect its diversity in this straightened world, Europe will have to become more united. To do so, Europeans will have to face two neuralgic questions. Where should the boundaries of this united Europe lie? How do they understand their civilization and the history that has shaped it? I turn to these questions in the next chapter.

# -V-

## WHICH BOUNDARIES? WHOSE HISTORY?

From my youth, I remember the last world war, and I know the value of the peace, stability and prosperity which we have today. . . . The wars and atrocities in former Yugoslavia have demonstrated what Europeans can do to each other when forces of disintegration are allowed to overtake the wish for unity. The enlargement of the European Union to me, therefore, is the fulfillment of a vision.

—Wim Kok, prime minister of the Netherlands, 2003

When European imperialists march to the east, they eventually lose in the west. The elastic is overstretched.

—Simon Jenkins, *Sunday Times*, June 2005

BOUNDARIES MATTER. They don't matter as much as they once did, but the notion that they have dwindled into mere lines on a map is an agreeable fantasy. Despite Google, You-Tube, Facebook, e-mails, iPods, cell phones, News International, McDonald's, Nike, Goldman Sachs, Madonna, climate change, international terrorism, the International Criminal Court, the Red Cross, and the English language, we do not live in a world without borders: try telling an immigration official or a customs officer that you don't carry a passport because you are a citizen of the world. Capital vaults over national frontiers, but the frontiers are still there to be vaulted over, and state policies help to determine the way in which it vaults.

Globalization did not descend like a Hayekian thunderbolt from a clear sky. It was the product of political choices by territorially bounded states, and states respond to it in different ways. In the academy, there is talk of cosmopolitan democracy, but it is a dream for the future, not a reality for the present.[1] Germs of a global civil society can be detected in worldwide climate change and anticapitalist protests, in smoothly suited Davos conferences of the World Economic Forum, and in global NGOs like Greenpeace and Médecins Sans Frontières, but so far they are nothing more than germs. Surprisingly large numbers of people think of themselves as global citizens,[2] but global citizenship, insofar as it exists, is an adjunct to national citizenship (and in Europe to EU citizenship as well), not the other way around. Political communities are bounded, and so is the European Union. Unlike most political communities in the developed world, however, the Union has experienced extraordinarily rapid and disorientating boundary changes in the space of a few years, and it is still reeling from the effects. These changes and effects have shaped the choices it now faces.

History matters too. Shared experiences, however blurred by time, fashion collective identities. Secular non-Zionist Jews, hostile to the policies of the Israeli state, are still marked at some deep level by the experience of the Holocaust, even if they were born after it happened. As Obama's election campaign showed, the scar of slavery and the memory of the Civil War still mark Americans, both white and black—however faintly in the case of the first. Nostalgia for the glories of the Caliphate surfaces today in the rhetoric of Osama bin Laden and Al Qaeda. And the shared experiences of the cape of Asia we call Europe live on, often in a distorted form, in the psyches of postmodern Europeans in the twenty-first century. To mention only a few examples, the Roman Empire, the schism between the Catholic and Orthodox churches, the Reformation, what used to be called "the expansion of Europe" and is now called imperialism, the French Revolution, the Bolshevik Revolution, and the two world wars have helped to make us what we are—even if we know nothing about them and are not conscious of their legacy.

Truisms? Of course, but truisms that are often forgotten in debates about the European Union and its future, and above all about its future extent. For the Union is a successful protest against boundaries and also against history. Part of the point of "uniting men" instead of states was to make national boundaries count for less, and eventually for very much less—not just in the relations between governments and firms, but in the lived experience of ordinary people. In a more complicated way, much the same is true of Monnet's second great dream: that of "exorcising the demons of the past." He did not want history to be forgotten. His vision was rooted in a particular, strongly held, and powerfully expressed interpretation of history. But he did look forward to a time when Europeans would no longer be the psychic prisoners of their history.

The process he envisaged was rather like Freudian psychotherapy. The patient (in other words, Europe) would confront its past, come to terms with it, and emerge free of complexes derived from it. A double ambition—to surmount boundaries and escape from history—has lain at the heart of the European project from the beginning. The growth of the original Community and subsequent Union—from six to nine, to twelve, to fifteen, to twenty-five, and now to twenty-seven—can be seen as a set of variations on these two themes. At each new stage in the process, a new set of boundaries succumbed to the Union's onward progress, like sand castles succumbing to a rising tide. Boundaries between its member states still exist, but they no longer run, like livid scars, across European imaginations. Today, the Rhine is just a river, the Pyrenees just a mountain range, the English Channel just a few miles of salt water. The demons of the past have not succumbed quite so easily. Danish and Polish resentments of Germany are still political forces to be reckoned with. So is British (or perhaps only English) resentment of what many Brits still call "Europe," as though Britain did not belong to it.

But despite the ugly outbreaks of xenophobia I mentioned in chapter 2, most of them directed against European Muslim minorities, not against their non-Muslim fellow Europeans, the successes are more remarkable than the setbacks—and much more remarkable than anyone could have expected when the European project was launched. The fact that the Irish Republic and the United Kingdom both belonged to the European Union undoubtedly made it easier for the Republic to delete its irredentist claim to Northern Ireland from its constitution, and for the British to declare explicitly that the province could secede from the United Kingdom if its people so wished. And the bloody history of the former Yugoslavia is a telling reminder of what might have happened to other ex-Communist countries if there had been no European Union to join. The ghost of Nicolas Chauvin, the (mythical) bombastic Napoleonic veteran immortalized in the word "chauvinist," has not quite vanished from the European scene, but he is less obtrusive than at any time since the French Revolution, perhaps since the emergence of the Westphalian state.

Yet the story is not quite as bland as this account implies. The Union has surmounted some boundaries but elevated others. The internal boundaries that divide its member states from each other bulk far smaller than they did when the European project was launched, but the external boundary that separates the entire Union from the outside world bulks larger. In the early days, when the European Community consisted only of the original "Six," the psychological and material differences between it and its northern neighbors, Britain and the Scandinavian countries, were less marked than those between its Mediterranean regions and the rest.

But as integration rolled on, and successive waves of enlargement swept the Union into territories that had once been closed to it, the boundary between Union Europe and non-Union Europe became ever-more obtrusive and, for the latter, ever-more galling. In 1990, the year following the peaceful revolution that breached the Berlin Wall, the formerly sovereign German Democratic Republic ceased to exist; its territories automatically became part of the European Union by virtue of their incorporation in the German Federal Republic. In 1995 the accession of Finland, Austria, and Sweden brought the total membership of the Union to fifteen. The Union now had common borders with Poland, the Czech Republic, Slovakia, Slovenia, Hungary, and (very nearly) with Estonia. Its eastern frontier had become a perceptual chasm, across which the unstable, impoverished, fate-buffeted, in some cases crime-ridden ex-Communist nations of East Central Europe had to contemplate an apparently rich, peaceful, law-abiding, often patronizing,[3] and above all *normal* other Europe. Their reaction mimicked those of Britain, Denmark, and Ireland in the 1970s and of Greece, Portugal, and Spain in the 1980s—but in spades. They wanted in. For them, there was nowhere else to go.

History with a capital *H* also wanted them in. The past whose demons Monnet had wanted to exorcise, the history he had wanted to get away from, was a history of militarism, totalitarianism, torture, genocide, and shame. But there was another history: a history of common values and a common civilization, of a cultured, cosmopolitan, liberal bourgeoisie moving easily between Paris, Vienna, Prague, Warsaw, and Berlin, and of a fertile, turbulent, pathbreaking intelligentsia, hugely enriched by emancipated Jews, that spanned the continent and even made occasional forays across the Channel. For the products of that civilization, the second quarter of the twentieth century had been a time, not just of suffering, but of anguish and incomprehension. It was as if they had been sundered from their pasts.

One example stands for many. Not long before he took his own life in Brazil, at the height of the Second World War, the celebrated Viennese Jewish novelist, playwright, and biographer Stefan Zweig wrote a haunting memoir of his life and times. The "volcanic eruptions" he had lived through, he wrote, had cut him off from "the past and all that it once comprised. . . . All the pale horses of the apocalypse have stormed through my life: revolution and famine, currency depreciation and terror, epidemics and emigration; I have seen great mass ideologies grow before my eyes and spread, Fascism in Italy, National Socialism in Germany, Bolshevism in Russia, and above all the ultimate pestilence that has poisoned the flower of our European culture, nationalism in general."[4]

Miraculously, however, the history that had molded Zweig and his counterparts all over Europe, and that they had helped to make, lived on in the dissident movements whose steady ideological tunneling beneath the Stalinoid regimes east of the iron curtain was one of the most remarkable themes of European history in the last quarter of the twentieth century. The astonishingly peaceful, sometimes almost consensual revolutions that eventually toppled the Communist rulers of East Central Europe had many authors.

Not the least of them was Mikhail Gorbachev, whose gallant, doomed attempt to "reconstruct" the Soviet Union itself did more than anything else to show that the Communist emperor no longer had clothes, and who rubbed the moral home by making it clear that the Red Army would no longer defend the Communist regimes outside the Soviet Union against their peoples.

But the dissidents of the region deserved at least as much of the credit. When Václav Havel, celebrated playwright and indomitable dissident, was elected as the first president of post-Communist Czechoslovakia, it was as if Zweig's Europe had been reborn. Europe, Havel told the European Parliament later, was a single entity. To believe that a democratic and stable Europe could forever coexist with an undemocratic and unstable one was like believing "that one half of a room could be heated and the other half kept un-heated."[5] When he and other former dissidents talked of "re-joining Europe," they were not thinking chiefly of the Europe of supermarkets, consumer durables, pineapples, and bananas, or even of the Euro-villages of Brussels, Strasbourg, and their arcane procedures. They were thinking of a Europe of the mind.

These yearnings were the demand side of the great enlargement to the east that transformed the European continent and the European Union in the first decade of the twenty-first century. The supply side was equally significant, perhaps even more so. Like all important EU initiatives, the enlargement process was driven by a confused medley of forces—some rooted in the perceived national interests of powerful member states, some in the institutional interests of the Brussels technocracy, some reflecting the attractions of a pool of cheap labor for "Old" European and particularly

German capital, and some stemming from a generous idealism that echoed the Monnet vision of the early days. German reunification made Germany by far the most populous
EU member state. It also made it a frontier state, bordering
Poland—the largest ex-Communist nation in the region—as
well as Czechoslovakia. For the newly reunited Germany,
peace, stability, and prosperity in its ex-Communist neighbors was a vital national interest.

As in previous enlargements, France was reticent, fear-
ing that "widening" would stymie "deepening." In the early
1990s the then French president François Mitterrand made
it clear he thought the ex-Communist states of East Central
Europe should be consigned to a diplomatic waiting room,
dignified with the question-begging appellation of "European Confederation," until 2010. From then until Chirac's
famous 2003 complaint that the prospective newcomers
from the east were "not well brought-up," that was a leitmo-
tiv of French policy.[6] As so often, the British started from
the same premise and reached a diametrically opposite conclusion. From the very beginning of the European project,
successive British governments had sought a loose-knit,
free-trading intergovernmental bloc in Europe, if possible
without supranational political institutions and certainly
without a federal dimension. To them, enlargement seemed
a boon. They too assumed that "widening" would stymie
"deepening," and they clamored for enlargement for that
reason.[7]

From these swirling currents emerged a rough, fluctuating consensus among EU member governments: the ex-
Communist countries would be allowed into the Union as
soon as they had shown they were fit for membership. But it
was the European Commission, not the member states, that
supplied the edge and drive needed to turn this consensus

into facts on the ground. For the Commission, enlargement was a heaven-sent opportunity. With the great adventure of a common currency virtually complete, it needed a mission; a cause; a juicy, meaty bone suited to technocratic teeth. Enlargement fit that prescription to perfection.

At a European summit in Copenhagen in the early nineties, the member governments agreed to a set of criteria— soon known as the "Copenhagen criteria"—which applicants for membership would have to satisfy in order to join. They would need stable institutions, guaranteeing democracy, the rule of law, and human rights. They would have to have functioning market economies, capable of coping with the competitive pressures emanating from the rest of the Union. Above all, they would have to adopt and implement the entire corpus of existing EU law, known in Brussels-speak as the *acquis communitaire*. It would be for the Commission to decide if these criteria had been satisfied; and it would be for Commission officials to make sure that they were. The result was a brilliantly conceived and brilliantly accomplished exercise in liberal imperialism—designed, in Jan Zielonka's words, to give the Union "control over developments in the post-Communist space."[8]

The Commission officials who drove it forward viewed their interlocutors in East Central Europe much as the British-dominated Indian Civil Service had viewed the native Indians under the Raj. One day they would be ready for membership. But that day had not yet come. In the meantime, they had to be brought up to scratch. They had to be taught democracy and market economics. They had to incorporate the thirty-five chapters and eighty thousand pages of existing Community law into their own laws. To do this, they had to submit to a meticulous program of reeducation, minutely monitored by emissaries from Brussels.

They had to unlearn the habits that they had learned under Communism and, in some cases, that they had inherited from their authoritarian, pre-Communist pasts. They had to learn new ones instead, and they had to convince persnickety examiners that they were doing so. They had to recast their institutions and construct a new economic and legal architecture. In some ways, the project was the most ambitious ever seen on the European continent. It was not the first attempt to remake European societies from above. Earlier ones included the Napoleonic revolution on horseback, the Nazi New Order, and the Stalinist revolutions from the turrets of the Red Army's tanks. But these had been backed by force and, in the last two cases, by secret police, prison camps, and torture chambers. The European Commission's revolution from above was backed only by the lure of Union membership, and of full participation in its decision making.

As I tried to show in previous chapters, the project succeeded beyond all reasonable expectation. Poland and Hungary applied for membership in 1994. They were followed by another eight former Communist countries in 1995 and 1996, making ten ex-Communist applicants in all. In 2004 eight of these ten became full members of the Union (together with Malta and Cyprus); in 2007 they were joined by Romania and Bulgaria. The benign imperialists of Brussels did not win control of the evolution of post-Communist space, exactly, but their role in shaping it was crucial. The countries located in that space did rejoin Europe, albeit on terms that presupposed their cultural and political inferiority to its existing citizens.

In management-speak, enlargement was a win-win process. Old Europe—the Carolingian Europe of the "Six," together with its outliers in the British Isles, Scandinavia, and the Iberian Peninsula[9]—had insured itself against trouble in its eastern borderlands. New Europe, the borderlands themselves, had secured a chance to share the prosperity and peace of Old Europe, and even to take part in its governance. It was a historic achievement, matching those of the founding fathers of the Union fifty years before.

Yet there was an absentee from the feast. Enlargement transformed the Union—irreversibly as well as dramatically. But the transformation was not confined to the newcomers from the east. Groucho Marx famously said that he wouldn't want to join a club that would have him as a member. He forgot to add that, if he did join, it would no longer be the same club. In just that sense, the post-enlargement Union was not the Union that the new members had sought to join—and not the Union that the old members had fashioned for themselves. The admission of twelve new member states and 100 million new citizens was a qualitative change in the Union's history at least as portentous as the Single European Act or the introduction of the euro. But it did not occur to the old member governments who fashioned the enlargement consensus, or to the Brussels technocrats who pushed it forward, to consult the citizens of the Union they were transforming and in whose names they claimed to be acting.

The European Parliament had to assent before negotiations with an applicant country could begin, and it did influence some of the details of the Commission's approach to the negotiations. But to equate assent by the European Parliament with assent by the Union's citizen body requires a heroic suspension of disbelief. It did not even occur to the governments to take the question to the court of public opinion—to encourage searching debate on the pros and cons in order to build a popular consensus for enlargement, buttressing the governmental consensus. There was no exercise in republican-style public reasoning, and only the flimsiest approximation to liberal-individualist accountability. "New" Europeans were given the chance to vote on the outcome of the accession negotiations in national referendums. "Old" Europeans had no chance to vote on the project, either at the end of the process or at the beginning. The end result of the whole exercise was a resounding victory for democracy and the rule of law—achieved in a scandalously undemocratic way.

It is hardly necessary to add that the great questions of civilization and territory—questions that the Union's founders had swathed in the necessary ambiguity described in chapter 2—were not seriously discussed. Mitterrand's hope that the ex-Communist countries in East Central Europe could be kept waiting for admission until well into the twenty-first century probably reflected his own approach to these questions. Deep down he did not believe that they and the Union's existing members belonged to a common civilization, and wished to exclude them from the territory that that civilization embraced. But he did not confront the question head-on; he seems to have hoped that, if it were ignored for long enough, it would go away.

The same was true of the proponents of enlargement. With her usual gutsy honesty, Margaret Thatcher might have relished a fight in support of the European credentials of the ex-Soviet satellites, but the last thing she would have wanted was a debate over the essentials of European civilization as such: it would have forced her to come clean about her attitudes to Britain's relationship with that civilization. In any case, she fell from power well before enlargement became a live issue. The leaders of the two weightiest countries in the enlargement camp—Gerhard Schroeder in Germany and Tony Blair in Britain—were not well equipped, to put it mildly, for a debate over fundamentals, and certainly not over these fundamentals. The same was true of the technocrats in the European Commission. The questions of civilization and territory were profoundly political and likely to prove highly divisive to boot. They were the kind of questions that technocrats instinctively run away from.

But now that almost all the ex-Communist countries outside the former Soviet Union are in the Union, the great questions hover like birds of prey on the edge of the European agenda. Who belongs to the Europe of the mind? *Is* there still a Europe of the mind? Assuming that "Europe" is more than a geographical expression, what makes it so? Is there a common European civilization? If so, what are its defining characteristics? Are there special European norms and practices that give meaning to the notion of a European ideal? If so, what are they? Above all, how far does the Europe that is more than a geographical expression extend?

Thanks, in part, to the success of the enlargement project of the 1990s and early 2000s, these questions tend to evoke a resounding silence or a pitying smile among Brussels technocrats and influential Brussels watchers. They seem slightly shocking or hopelessly naïve. In any case, they are politically incorrect. Enlargement was a triumph; that is all anyone needs to know. Tiresome questions about the nature and limits of Europe might imply that the triumph was not as glorious as it seemed. Besides, a focus on civilizations has become suspect—in part, for good reasons. It smacks of the glib, neoconservative determinism of Samuel P. Huntington's theory that the post–cold war world was bound to be structured by an unavoidable "clash" between historically determined civilizations, above all between "Western" civilization on the one hand and "Sinic" and "Muslim" civilizations on the other.[10]

But the flaw in Huntington's theory was its determinism, not its focus on civilization. The fashionable talk among the many Commission officials and Brussels watchers who ignore the role of civilizations altogether is equally glib and a lot more hubristic. It is about Europe's soft power; about the transformative effects of EU membership, or even the mere prospect of EU membership, on new members or candidates for membership. Europe is part savior and part moral crusader. Its mission is to spread democracy and the rule of law to its "near-abroad" by holding out the promise of membership in return for democratic reform and economic liberalization. By implication, at least, its vocation is therefore continuous enlargement, from one near-abroad to the next: yesterday the East Balkans; tomorrow, the West Balkans; then Turkey; after Turkey, Ukraine; and, for the really wide-eyed, after Ukraine, Belarus, Moldova, Georgia, and Armenia and perhaps (who knows?) Russia and, conceivably, even Israel. Deepening is for the birds; widening is all. The rationale is that, in our postmodern world, soft power trumps hard power, or in more elevated language that Kant trumps Hobbes.[11]

To put it at its lowest, this is a dangerous oversimplification. "Soft power" is a slippery concept; and in real life the distinction between it and "hard power" is apt to slither into a bog of semantic confusion. For the Harvard political scientist, Joseph S. Nye Jr., who coined the term, soft power "rests on the ability to set the political agenda in a way that shapes the preferences of others." Fundamental to that ability are "intangible power resources such as an attractive culture, ideology and institutions."[12] Nye's thesis pinpoints an important truth, which old-fashioned realists too often ignore. Intangible power resources undoubtedly matter; so does the capacity to set the political agenda. The great empires of the past, from the Roman to the British, have all sought to embed their cultures, ideologies, and institutions in the minds and hearts of their subjects. But the role of soft power in Nye's sense has been much more limited than the EU champions of continuous enlargement admit.

In one perspective, the crowds that thronged the squares of Leipzig and Prague and made the velvet revolutions of 1989 were using soft power. They changed the political agenda and made possible what had hitherto seemed impossible. They did so because the regimes they toppled had lost faith in their own ideologies and had no answer to the ideological challenge of the insurgents. But that was not the only reason why the velvet revolutionaries won. Another was that the ruler of the Soviet Union chose not to use its hard power to crush them; and he made his choice of his own free will, not because he had been constrained by EU or American soft power.

The Chinese students who attempted to deploy soft power in Tiananmen Square were brutally crushed by the regime's hard power. The success of the then European Community in the postwar period can fairly be attributed to soft power. But had there been no American hard power in the background, it is doubtful if the European project could ever have been launched. Mahatma Gandhi was perhaps the twentieth century's supreme exemplar of soft power in action, but as he himself acknowledged, his success in using it depended on British willingness to allow him to do so. He would not have got very far if India had been ruled by the Nazis. Kant trumps Hobbes only if the other players are at least proto-Kantians. As Robert Kagan has forcefully pointed out,[13] this is rarely true of the naughty world beyond the European liberal empire.

The successful use of soft power depends on at least a modicum of shared values and assumptions between subjects and objects, users and used-upon. That was true of Gandhi and the British; it was even more true of the European Commission and the post-Communist regimes in East Central Europe. The Commission's behavior toward the candidate EU members there was quite rough. In its dealings with them, the Commission had the whip hand. They were desperate to join; and once they had embarked on the journey to membership, it was virtually impossible for them to draw back. It didn't negotiate with them, in any normal sense of the word; it told them what they had to do.

But in the last resort, it and they both belonged to the same Europe of the mind, and all the parties to the exercise knew that. The former Communist satellites wanted to rejoin Europe, to become normal Europeans after half a century of abnormality; and, albeit with occasional misgivings, they accepted the Commission's view of what normality meant. No one used soft power to persuade them. No one needed to. Once they were no longer coerced by Soviet hard power, they were free to do what they had always longed to do. It does not follow that, because the Europe of the mind embraced East Central Europe, it must also embrace the territories beyond the EU's new borders. To assume, without careful thought and solid evidence, that it necessarily does so would be an evasion of responsibility.

The vision of an endlessly expanding European Union, marching eastward to the Caucasus, purports to be new, but like many purportedly new visions, it is in fact hoary with age. It is a new version of the dogmatic universalist rationalism of the French eighteenth-century Enlightenment and of the quintessentially antipolitical mentality of the latter-day Saint-Simonians I mentioned in chapter 2. It assumes that everyone knows what democracy is and agrees about its meaning: that democracy means the same thing in Tokyo as in Toronto, in Baghdad as in Birmingham. It also assumes that words on paper can change realities on the ground: that if a given government signs up to democratic reform, open markets, and the rule of law, and subjects itself to vigilant scrutiny by apolitical technicians from Brussels, all these changes will come to pass.

It focuses entirely on the aspirations of potential candidates for membership and pays no attention to the likely effect of their admission on the Union's cohesion and political capacities, or to the democratic right of existing EU citizens to decide whether yet more new members should be admitted and yet more disruptive changes undergone. It views Union membership as a sort of good conduct prize, to be awarded to congenial and supposedly deserving pupils, without asking what they are likely to do with the prize once they have received it. It forgets that democracies can be as self-centered and uncooperative as authoritarian regimes and that democracy is a culture as well as a set of institutions. It assumes that the thin bonds of market exchange and individual rights will suffice to hold an ever-expanding Union together. All too often, it is a form of psychological displacement activity, giving the EU a warm glow of moral self-satisfaction while diverting it from the harsh and pressing questions of effective governance and democratic legitimacy. Above all, it wishes away tradition, habit, and *difference*. It is Huntington through the looking glass—history as irrelevant lumber in place of history as a determinate cage.

To be fair, there is an element of truth in the vision. It is certainly true that the European Community and later the

European Union were magnets for successive near-abroads. Each of the enlargements of the last fifty years is proof of that. It is also true that slow, patient, culturally sensitive work on the ground may, over time, help to nurture democratic "habits of the heart" in particular places and particular institutions where local people are receptive to them.[14] But this has nothing to do with Kantian universalism or hubristic dreams of EU soft power. It is modest, bottom-up pluralism in action, carried out in the spirit of the Latin saying *festina lente* (make haste slowly).

In principle, any European state can apply for EU membership. But the principle is not as clear as it looks. Europeans have never been sure quite who they are or quite where they live. According to the famous Greek myth of Europa and the bull, our story begins (perhaps appropriately, in view of some horrifying later chapters) with an abduction and a rape. Zeus, in the guise of a white bull, ravished the beautiful Phoenician princess, Europa, and carried her on his back while he swam across the seas to the island of Crete. There she gave birth to the dreaded Minotaur, half man and half bull. The British historian Norman Davies suggests that the myth reflects the Greeks' debt to the far older civilization of ancient Egypt, whose orbit included Phoenicia, and captures "the essential restlessness" of Mediterranean civilization, with its maritime emphasis and endless questing, in contrast to the more durable but also more lethargic river valley civilizations of Asia.[15]

Be that as it may, the Greeks undoubtedly saw the narrow strip of sea that links the Black Sea to the Aegean, by way of the Bosphorus, the Sea of Marmora, and the Dardanelles, as a clear demarcation line between Europe and Asia Minor (today's Anatolia) and bequeathed that definition to later Europeans. That boundary is still sharply defined and undisputed today. So are Europe's maritime and oceanic boundaries to its north, west, and south: that was one of the reasons why Morocco's application to join the Union was turned down in short order. But trouble comes in the territories to the north of the Bosphorus, where Europe merges into the vast Eurasian plain to its east.

For Herodotus, the boundary between Europe and Asia was the River Don, which flows for twelve hundred miles from Novomoskovsk, south of Moscow, to the Sea of Azov, adjacent to the Black Sea. For a long time, that was the prevailing European view. But in the eighteenth century, a Swedish officer serving in the Russian army, by the name of Strahlenberg, defined a new boundary, more flattering to his European-oriented Russian masters: the low hills dignified by the name "Ural Mountains." Strahlenberg's boundary has held the field ever since: when Charles de Gaulle said that Europe extends from the Atlantic to the Urals, he was, for once, expressing a consensus view.

Unfortunately, the consensus view was, and is, preposterous. Were it taken seriously, Tbilisi and Baku would count as European cities, and even Tehran would have at least a faint claim to that status as well. A chunk of what is now Kazakhstan would be part of Europe, and so might smaller parts of Uzbekistan and Turkmenistan. And wherever Europe may or may not end, Russia most definitely does not end at the Urals. On the contrary, it stretches right across the Eurasian land mass to the Pacific Ocean. The formula "Europe from the Atlantic to the Urals" makes western Russia European, and Siberia Asian. But Siberia is part of Russia and has been settled by Russians, voluntarily as well as involuntarily, for several centuries. Tobolsk, the earliest Russian settlement in Siberia, was settled twenty years before the first English colonists in the New World arrived in Jamestown, Virginia.

In truth, geography cannot provide answers to the great questions. Europe is less a continent, like Asia or Africa, than a subcontinent, like India. But unlike India, it has no Himalayas. The boundary between it and the rest of the Eurasian land mass is not a fixed, unchanging, universally recognizable geographical fact. It is a mental construct, impalpable, shifting, and above all, contestable. To treat Strahlenberg's arbitrary frontier as a given is cartographic fetishism.

Among other things, this is a way of saying that Europe's boundary problem is also a problem for Russia—and therefore for the non-Russian successor states of the Soviet Union that once belonged to the Tsarist Empire and now fringe the EU's eastern borders. A central theme of European history from the late seventeenth century to the mid-twentieth was Russia's (and later the Soviet Union's) westward expansion. From the time of Catherine the Great in the late eighteenth century to that of Gorbachev in the late twentieth, first Imperial Russia and then the Soviet Union were important, and sometimes critically important, players in European politics. But as I suggested in the prologue, the Russians have never been sure who or where *they* are. Is Russia part of Europe or not? If it is part of Europe, in what sense is it European? The Third Rome, heir to the glories of Byzantium, or a recruit for the European Enlightenment? Stalin's Socialism in one country or Trotsky's world revolution? Brezhnev's inward-looking stagnation or Gorbachev's outward-looking perestroika? The murdered investigative journalist Anna Politovskaya or the former KGB officer Vladimir Putin? Russians have never been able to make up their minds, and their uncertainty has fed into Europe's.

Russia's high culture is certainly European. The land of Pushkin, Gogol, Chekhov, Tolstoy, Dostoyevsky, Pasternak, and Solzhenitsyn—or for that matter of Tchaikovsky, Borodin, and Shostakovich—belongs to the same cultural universe as those of Shakespeare and Dickens, or of Goethe and Thomas Mann, or of Racine and Proust. Indeed, its place in that universe is more secure than those of many former Communist countries in East Central Europe that now belong to the European Union. But Russia's high culture is both European and not European. The same is true of that other European offshoot, the United States, the land of Whitman, Melville, Pound, and Robert Frost. In the last few years, talented Indian writers have produced some of the most glittering new novels written in the English language. But that does not mean that European civilization now encompasses India. What it does mean is that high cultures are transgressive. They learn from each other, sometimes without realizing it, and they also borrow from each other.

Political culture is different; and political culture is the prism through which the debate over Europe's eastern borders should be viewed. Here, Russia's path has been cruelly different from the European norm. Poor soil, vast distances, dense forests, and a harsh climate fostered extensive slash-and-burn cultivation in contrast to the intensive agriculture of Europe proper. When the soil was exhausted, the cultivators moved on, contributing to a drift of population toward the east and south. Expanding frontiers and porous boundaries had to be defended; defense depended on conscript forces raised by strong, autocratic rulers. Another source of Russian exceptionalism was the Mongol invasions of the thirteenth century. Muscovy, the heart of Russia, began as an obscure principality whose rulers acted in effect as tax collectors for despotic Mongol Khans. The Muscovite princes aped their Mongol overlords as well as serving them. Little by little, Muscovy overcame the other Russian principalities in the area; in the late fifteenth century, the reigning Muscovite prince gradually and cautiously began to assume the title of Tsar, or Caesar.

But the Russian tsar had more in common with a Mongol Khan than with a European king, or even emperor. He was the absolute, personal ruler of an ever-expanding "patrimonial state,"[16] whose economic and political life he controlled and whose elites depended on his favor. There were no rival sources of legitimate power, no equivalent to the jumble of medieval Europe that I mentioned in chapter 2, and no social spaces where a European-style civil society could take root.[17]

Until the seventeenth century, the Russian state's astonishing land hunger was directed eastward. By 1700 the tsar's domains fringed the Chinese empire and the Pacific Ocean. But a change of focus came in the eighteenth century. Russia ceased to be an overwhelmingly Asiatic power and became a European one as well—a change epitomized in 1814, when victorious Russian troops, fresh from vanquishing Napoleon's Grande Armée, marched in triumph down the Champs Elysées in Paris. (Not even Stalin's Red Army could boast as much.) But though Russia was in Europe, it was not of Europe. The Russian state was still, in essence, a patrimonial state. The tsar was still the absolute, unchecked autocrat of all his dominions. Despite a marvelously inventive and spirited intelligentsia, there was still no equivalent to a European civil society. For a brief decade and a half at the beginning of the twentieth century, it looked as if Russia might overcome its past and evolve into a liberal democracy, but the Bolshevik putsch in November 1917 snuffed out such hopes.

Stalin's Soviet Union was the old patrimonial state writ large, with no private property rights and no civil society, ruled by an unchecked autocrat. In democracies, the state is supposed to be the servant of the people. Under Soviet Communism, as under the tsars, the people were servants of the state. Fifty-seven years after Stalin's death, and 426 years after the death of the arch-patrimonial ruler, Tsar Ivan the Terrible, the shadow of that state still lies heavily on the truncated Russia that emerged from the collapse of the Soviet Union. Less obviously, it lies as heavily on the other former Soviet republics, erstwhile domains of the Russian tsars and later of Stalin's patrimonial state, which emerged with it.

At this point, a great unmentionable (at least in present-day Europe) rears its head: religion. For the great French historian Fernand Braudel, civilizations were shaped by collective mentalities or habits of mind, "transmitted from generation to generation." At the heart of these habits was religion—the "strongest feature" of this crucial dimension of all civilizations. This was most obviously true of non-European civilizations, Braudel thought. But it was also true, albeit less obviously, of the "West," where even atheists had been marked by the legacy of Christianity and the "serene or stormy dialogue" between laicism, science, and religion.[18]

In recent years, as I tried to show in chapter 3, storms have been more noticeable than serenity. A notable example occurred during the long-drawn-out negotiations over the abortive EU Constitutional Treaty. A group of largely Catholic EU member states, including Poland, Italy, and the Czech Republic, backed by the Vatican and Angela Merkel, famously the daughter of a Protestant pastor in the then

Communist German Democratic Republic, sought to include an explicit reference to Europe's Christian heritage in the preamble. They lost what became a quite bitter battle. Nicolas Sarkozy, self-appointed champion of the French tradition of laïcité, and Tony Blair, future Catholic convert but champion of eventual Turkish entry to the Union, joined forces to defeat them. The eventual text made a mealy-mouthed reference to Europe's "cultural, religious and humanist inheritance," which was subsequently carried over to the Lisbon Treaty. No one pointed out that Erasmus, the greatest humanist of them all, was an ordained Christian priest or that Europe's cultural inheritance, from the soaring Gothic cathedrals of northern France to Bach's cantatas, is saturated with Christian themes. The long centuries of the Christian presence in Europe, with all its glories and horrors, had been consigned to an oubliette.

And not only the Christian presence. All three of the Abrahamic religions—Judaism, Christianity, and Islam—have helped to shape the Europe of the twenty-first century, not least through their complex and sometimes fraught encounters with each other. Jewish and Muslim critiques persuaded Christian theologians to hone their arguments; the first Christian universities were modeled on the great Muslim university of Al-Azhar in Cairo. Commentaries on Aristotle by the Muslim philosopher Averroës (Ibn Rushd) and the Jewish philosopher Maimonides (Musa ibn Maymun) left an enduring impression on Christian thought, by way of the disputatious theologians of the University of Paris.[19] And as Braudel implied, the nonreligious and antireligious strands in European civilization are incomprehensible if their religious targets are left out of the reckoning. Without belief, unbelief would make no sense: Nietzsche could not have proclaimed the death of God if no one had ever thought God lived. An attempt to sever European civilization from its religious roots would be an exercise in cultural lobotomy.

This applies above all to the centuries-old gulf between Orthodox Christianity on the one hand and both Catholic and Protestant Christianity on the other. In Catholic Christendom, the relationship between spiritual and temporal power was often tense and sometimes fraught with bitterness and mutual contempt. The pope was not just the heir of St. Peter, whom Christ had chosen to be the rock on which his Church would be built; he was Christ's vicar on earth, God's ambassador and representative. He could, and frequently did, excommunicate secular rulers who disputed his authority. Famously, Pope Gregory VII kept the excommunicate emperor Henry IV waiting for three days in the snow outside the castle of Canossa before granting him absolution.

But papal claims ran up against the claims of secular rulers, above all those of the so-called Holy Roman emperors, the supposed heirs of Charlemagne. Neither ecclesiastical nor secular power reigned supreme; Catholic Europe was a complex, fluctuating "constellation of jurisdictions."[20] The Protestant Reformation added to the constellation and exacerbated the complexity. Diversity (and confusion) was the rule. Church and state were not separate, exactly, but neither controlled the other.

Orthodox Europe took a very different path. In Byzantium, the chief citadel of Orthodoxy until the Ottomans conquered it, the secular power of the emperor and the ecclesiastical power of the Orthodox patriarch were combined in a single "coherent authority."[21] After the fall of Byzantium in 1453 CE, Moscow gradually took its place as the center of the Orthodox communion. It was the "third Rome," proclaimed its churchmen; and there would never be a fourth.

The self-proclaimed Russian "tsar" Ivan III saw himself as the heir of the Byzantine emperors and appropriated the Byzantine double-headed eagle as the symbol of his realm. Later tsars claimed descent from the first Roman emperor, Augustus—a claim echoed from pulpits throughout the land. In religious terms, at least, Russia became a coarser version of Byzantium. Spiritual and temporal power fused into a church-state, effectively controlled by the tsars. It did not have everything its own way. Liturgical changes in the seventeenth century provoked a schism with "Old Believers" who seceded from what they saw as a corrupted institution. But there was no serious ecclesiastical challenge to the Russian version of Byzantium's "coherent authority." In religious as in secular matters, the pluralism of western Christendom was absent.

In the light of all this, what are we to make of the great questions of civilization and territory? How should Europeans answer the questions "What does it mean to be a European?" and "Where does Europe end?" *Can* they answer them? Two traps lie in wait. One is the ultraliberal assumption (more often tacit than explicit) that autonomous, unanchored individuals choose their identities for themselves, without reference to shared histories or common cultures. The other is the Huntingtonian determinism that pictures civilizations as unchanging, monolithic, all-embracing psychic prisons whose denizens behave as the civilization has programmed them to behave.

In truth, civilizations do exist, but they also develop and change. They collide with each other, and they borrow from each other. Muslim Spain is a breathtaking example, but so are present-day Europe, India, and America. Civilizations and the cultures that compose them are sites of disputation, contestation, and conflict, not just between them but within the souls of their members. The answers to my questions can never be more than provisional. What one generation thinks it has settled, a succeeding generation may reopen.

The search for a definitive European identity and a permanent answer to the question of what Europe means is, in fact, a wild goose chase. Identities are not freely chosen in some historyless nirvana, but they cannot be imposed, even by mass conversion. Nor are they matters of blood and soil, or unquestioned traditions. Traditions help to make us what we are, but they are never unquestioned: they have to be interpreted and reinterpreted in the light of changing circumstances. The contestation I mentioned a moment ago is of their essence. Shared identities are always in flux. Those who lose the argument today may win it tomorrow: debates over slavery, women's suffrage, and much later over gay rights are good examples.

But that is not a reason for avoiding my questions. Europeans cannot afford to shuffle on forever, without knowing where they are going or where they want to go. And the questions are supremely political as well as urgent. They are inextricably entangled with the patently political questions of government and authority discussed in the previous chapter. They can't be answered by bureaucrats, or technocrats, or think tankers, or even governments. Answers contrived in the European village in Brussels—or, for that matter, in the Westminster village in London or the Elysée village in Paris—will carry no conviction. Here too open and searching public debate is long overdue. Only the people of Europe can decide who they are.

So far, the European Union has sedulously avoided a serious debate about the nature and limits of European civilization. The pace and extent of EU enlargement have been determined ad hoc, in response to immediate pressures: the threat of Communism in post-Salazar Portugal, the danger that post-Fascist Greece might leave NATO, and above all the velvet revolutions in East Central Europe. The one big exception is de Gaulle's decision to exclude Britain on the grounds that she was not truly European—a decision that provoked indignation in Britain but turned out to be salutary for the British, who were forced to ask hard questions about the kind of people *they* were.

But ad hocery is no longer adequate. Before long, the Union of twenty-seven, procured by the latest enlargement, is virtually certain to take in the seven nations of the West Balkans that nestle between Greece, Bulgaria, and Slovenia. They can hardly be left as an impoverished and resentful fistful of states, bordered by EU member states to the north, east, and south and by the Adriatic Sea to the west. Battered, chastened Iceland may well join them. But once that enlargement is over, the questions of principle that the Union has dodged for so long will have to be answered—provisionally, to be sure, but firmly and clearly. The alternative is more ad hoc capitulations to immediate, factitious pressures, each distracting the Union from the central problems of how to democratize its constitution and legitimize its institutions, and how to halt its slide into global irrelevance.

The debate should begin by revisiting the shared experiences that have made present-day Europe what it is. Not all of them were pretty, to put it mildly. Their dark side—not just the Holocaust and the Gulag, but a long list of ethnic hatreds, savage wars, cruel tortures, and mass killings—should not be airbrushed out of the story. They are to European civilization what slavery and the genocide of the Native Americans are to America's. For their own sakes even more than for Europe's, the perpetrator nations need to confront their pasts and come to terms with them, in the way that postwar federal Germany did and that postwar France took a long time to do. This is not easy: perpetrators of some horrors were often victims of others. Even Germany was a victim, as well as a perpetrator, as I tried to show in chapter 2; and so, on a massive scale, was the Soviet Union.

However, trading victimhoods is a dangerous pastime. What matters is that certain experiences, some good, some bad, and some morally indifferent, hold the key to the great questions Europeans now face. Any list of these experiences will be contestable. But paramount candidates clearly include the inconclusive medieval struggle between spiritual and temporal power; the schism between Byzantine Orthodoxy and Roman Catholicism; the Protestant Reformation and the wars of religion; the failure of successive attempts to unite Europe by force, from Charlemagne to Hitler; and the remarkable longevity of medieval Europe's jumble of principalities, duchies, baronies, bishoprics, and free cities.

Their legacy is summed up in the Union's motto: United in Diversity. The theme goes a long way back. Brooding on the moral of his story, Edward Gibbon, the great eighteenth-century British historian of the decline and fall of the Roman Empire, singled out diversity and the freedom it protected as fundamental features of the Europe of his day. Europe, he wrote, was "one great republic." But because power was divided between its constituent parts instead of being concentrated at the center, there was no need to fear that it would succumb to a single despot as the Roman Republic had done. The "abuses of tyranny" were restrained "by the mutual influence of fear and shame." Republics had acquired "order and stability"; monarchies had "imbibed the principles of freedom, or, at least, of moderation."[22] Gibbon wrote more than two hundred years ago, but his elegant prose still captures the special quality of European civilization. Diversity is of its essence.

A comparison with the United States may help. What strikes European visitors to the United States most of all is its *sameness.* The French nobleman Alexis de Tocqueville, perhaps the most perceptive of all European visitors to America, went there in 1831, with some forebodings. He thought democracy would eventually prevail in his own country as well as in America, and he feared that it might snuff out liberty. He returned reassured: thanks to the vitality of its civil associations, liberty was safe in democratic America. But he was struck by the uniformity of American public opinion. It seemed to permeate "the thinking of everyone by a sort of enormous pressure of the mind of all upon the individual intelligence." The dissenting individual was "very near acknowledging that he is wrong when the greater number of his countrymen assert that he is so."[23] And there was a danger that this instinctive uniformity might breed a new and subtle kind of despotism—a "regular, quiet and gentle" servitude in which "the will of man is not shattered, but softened, bent, and guided."[24]

De Tocqueville's insight still resonates today, with American critics of their own civilization, and even more with European visitors. (A good example of the former is the gloom-laden, once famous 1950 study of conformism in American suburbs, *The Lonely Crowd,* in which David Riesman, Nathan Glazer, and Reual Denney anatomized what they called the "other-directed" personality, which was allegedly replacing the robust "inner-directed" personality of America's great days.) Of course, there are huge differences within America—between subcultures, between geographical regions, between cities. But to European eyes, the way of life still seems extraordinarily uniform. San Francisco, or even Phoenix, Arizona, seem closer to New York than Taranto to Milan or Madrid to Barcelona. The homogenizing pressures of the global marketplace are at work even in Europe, but as I argued in chapter 3, they are offset by the rebirth of ancient provinces and the reassertion of old identities, which have no American parallels.

With diversity goes pluralism. It is easy to confuse European pluralism with American individualism, but the two are different. The American Dream is one of *individuals*, striving for individual success and making the most of their individual talents. The European ideal is one of *groups*, living together in harmony, negotiating their differences, and nurturing their members. Of course, both Dream and ideal are repeatedly flouted in practice, but that does not weaken their hold on the relevant public cultures. Not least, they help to explain the subtle differences between American-style neoliberalism and the more collectivist economic approaches of continental Europe. (At first sight, the United Kingdom seems closer to the United States than is the rest of the European Union, but here, as in many other respects, the English Channel is, in reality, a good deal narrower than the Atlantic.)

More to the point, European pluralism has nothing in common with the centuries-old authoritarianism of the Russian imperial state and its manifold successors. As I argued a moment ago, that tradition was incarnated in the Soviet state for seventy years after the Bolshevik seizure of power in 1917. Not surprisingly, its legacy is still omnipresent in former tsarist and Soviet territories today. That means that it is much more widespread than casual "Western" observers are apt to think. It is now incarnated, not only in the Russian Federation itself, but also in the non-Russian republics that were ruled by despotic tsars before the revolution and by even more despotic Communists thereafter, and that now fringe Russia's western and southern borders. Tsar Putin was not a reincarnation of Tsar Stalin or Tsar Nicholas, but he was still a tsar. President Medvedev may or may not become a tsar, but Tsar Putin still lurks behind him.

Russian authoritarianism has little immediate bearing on the questions of civilization and territory with which the European Union now faces. Few dispute that the Russian state is as authoritarian as ever, and no one—certainly not Russia's rulers—thinks it should be admitted to the EU. (It is, however, a member of the Council of Europe.) But in two other former Soviet republics, Belarus and Ukraine, matters are more complicated. Belarus, part of the Russian empire long before it became a Soviet republic, may not have a tsar, but it certainly has a mini-tsar—the sometime opponent of the dissolution of the Soviet Union, Alexander Lukashenko. It has been banned from the Council of Europe on the grounds that its regime does not respect democratic norms. Ukraine, sharply divided between its Russian-oriented east and its Europe-oriented west, has no tsar—at least, not at present. But it had mini-tsars for almost a decade and a half after the fall of the Soviet Union. One of them, Victor Yanukovych, was recently elected president.

For a magic moment, many overenthusiastic Western observers saw Ukraine's so-called Orange Revolution of 2004 as a victory for people power, like the velvet revolutions in East Central Europe. Yet there is not much sign of people power in the Byzantine and murky politics of Ukraine today. They have recently been dominated by a personal battle for power, of labyrinthine complexity, between Yanukovych and another would-be mini-tsar, the ultra-rich former oligarch and so-called gas princess, Yulia Tymoshenko. As for the culture of democracy, the global Corruption Perceptions Index shows that Ukraine is as corrupt as Zimbabwe and Sierra Leone (and for that matter as Russia) and far more corrupt than any existing EU member state.[25]

Turkey, the other truncated former imperial power that borders Europe and haunts the European imagination, has a different story but an equally problematic one. Most of the shared experiences that made Europe what it is passed Turkey by: many were of bloodthirsty quarrels between different Christian confessions, which had few echoes in a Muslim-ruled empire. For many centuries, Ottoman Turkey was Europe's Other—in the early-modern period a menacing predator, and in the nineteenth and early twentieth centuries an overripe fruit for the plucking. ("The sick man of Europe," in the parlance of the day.) The two other great land empires of the region, Austria-Hungary and Russia, vied for pickings with each other, as did Turkey's successor states, Greece, Bulgaria, Serbia, and Romania. The murder of the Austrian archduke Ferdinand that sparked the First World War was a product of these rivalries.

Then Europe became Turkey's Other. Modern Turkey was formed by virtual expulsion from Europe, in the years immediately before and after the First World War. Expulsion was followed by mimicry. Kemal Atatürk, the founder of the post-Ottoman Turkish state, launched a ferocious project of top-down modernization, with echoes of Peter the Great's Russia, Meiji Japan, and Mussolini's Italy. It had two dimensions—ethnic nationalism in the central European mold and an aggressive secularism reminiscent of Third Republic France. The second failed. Turkey remains an overwhelmingly Muslim country and, as in the United States (though not in most of western Europe), the political impact of religion seems stronger today than it used to be. Ethnic nationalism, however, seems as obdurate as it was under Atatürk.

In one distinctly unpleasant respect, Turkey was an innovator. The genocide inflicted on its Armenian minority was the first great genocide of the twentieth century. Today, it is governed by a moderate Islamist party, at loggerheads with the secularist-Kemalist establishment, entrenched in the army and the courts. It seeks entry to the European Union, and desultory negotiations are in progress in Brussels. Turkey is unquestionably a democracy but an essentially tribal democracy—a democracy for Turks, not for the Kurdish minority. And the Turkish state has signally failed to come to terms with the genocide of the Armenians, in the way that the postwar West German state came to terms with the Holocaust.

It is time to pull the threads together. Thread number one is unmistakable. History trumps geography. The intangibles of memory and culture matter more than the delusive certainties of mapmaking. The EU's great enlargement to the east was a victory for the Europe of the mind—for peoples desperate to "rejoin" a Europe from which totalitarian regimes had cut them off. But, apart from the area of western Ukraine that once belonged to the Hapsburg Empire (an important exception, it must be said), the enlarged Union's eastern neighbors cannot rejoin Europe: they did not belong to Europe in the first place. They are European geographically, but it is hard to argue that they are part of the Europe of the mind.

In essence the same is true of Turkey, though for much more complex reasons than opponents of Turkish entry usually emphasize. Turkey's poverty would certainly pose problems for the Union, but they could be overcome. Her Muslim faith—the real reason why the prospect of Turkish membership makes many existing EU citizens shudder—is, if anything, an argument in her favor. It would show beyond doubt that Europe is the child of all three Abrahamic religions, and not just of two; and it would underline the diversity that is of Europe's essence. The problem with Turkey is not that it is Muslim but that it is one of the last redoubts of ethnic nationalism in the region; that, as a Council official in Brussels put it to me some time ago, "Turkey is modern, but Europe is postmodern." Atatürk's aggressively secularist legacy is the problem, not Muhammad's religious one.

True, "never say never" is as good a rule for commentators as it is for statesmen. The struggle between westerners and easterners within Ukraine's troubled soul may end in victory for the former. It is conceivable that Turkey will abandon ethnic nationalism and tribal democracy and embrace European pluralism. But neither of these things is likely to happen anytime soon.

The second thread is more convoluted, but it is not difficult to trace. Post-enlargement Europe is like a lanky schoolboy who has outgrown his strength. Its reach patently exceeds its grasp. Despite a population of 500 million and a total GDP of more than $16 trillion, it speaks with too many voices to carry conviction. It was marginalized at Copenhagen, it has had no significant impact on the conflict between Israel and Palestine, and it is a prey to Russia's energy blackmail. Diverse it undoubtedly is, and gloriously so. United it patently is not, to the great detriment of its citizens. To become yet more diverse before first becoming more united would be an act of irresponsible folly that the next generation of Europeans might find it hard to forgive.

The last thread is more complex. Alexis de Tocqueville famously sought a "new political science for a new world": that was the point of his visit to America. The new world he had in mind was democracy. In some ways it was alarming, perhaps even threatening, but there was no point in bemoaning its advent. It was the inescapable wave of the future. To come to terms with it and make the best of it, the old world, to which de Tocqueville himself belonged, had to see it as it really was, without preconceptions or prejudices. Largely without recognizing it, twenty-first-century Americans and Europeans are now living through a Tocquevillian moment.

The world in which most of today's American and European adults grew up—the world structured by Kipling's imperialistic certitudes, by dim memories of the glory that was Greece, by the American dream of a "city on a hill," by the myth of "Judaeo-Christian civilization" and the countermyth of a monolithic "Western" Enlightenment, by the teleologies of Marxism, liberalism, and allegedly scientific rationalism—is vanishing as surely as did the ancien régimes of eighteenth- and early nineteenth-century Europe. The infinitely more complex world that our children and grandchildren will live in, a world on which the language and assumptions of "West" versus "East" will have no purchase, is already edging it aside. Coming to terms with this new world will involve a profound change of mentality and self-understanding—as profound as the changes that the upper classes of Europe had to make in order to come to terms with the arrival of democracy.

To take just a few examples, we, the "westerners" of yesteryear, will have to stop thinking of science and rationality as "Western" inventions. We shall have to put the (Indian) inventors of Arabic numerals in our pantheon alongside the Greek inventors of geometry, and Ibn Rushd alongside Aristotle. We shall have to abandon our self-centered and patronizing belief that democracy and free discussion were exported to a backward "East" by a progressive "West," and reconstruct our mental universe to take account of the indigenous Indian tradition of public reasoning and religious toleration that long antedated the "Western" presence in the subcontinent.[26] More generally, we shall have to recognize that the familiar "Western" narrative of global history, in which uniquely precious and, in evolutionary terms, uniquely successful "Western" values molded the modern world in our great-grandparents' image, is a parochial distortion of a far more complex truth. And, on a less elevated but more immediate level, we shall have to accept that the "West" will never again call the shots in global politics: that there is no longer a "West" to call them.

The great question now facing Europe, whether as idea or as fact, is not the impact of the economic crisis, the future of the Eurozone, or the admission or nonadmission of new member states, important as these are. It is how to grow a European demos that can sustain a European federation, playing a worthy part in such a world.

# NOTES

<hr/>

## 1. Prologue

1. Robert Kagan, *The Return of History and the End of Dreams* (London: Atlantic Books, 2008); Robert Cooper, *The Breaking of Nations: Order and Chaos in the Twenty-first Century* (London: Atlantic Books, 2004); and Philip Bobbit, *Terror and Consent: The Wars for the Twenty-first Century* (London: Allen Lane, 2008).

2. Quoted in Roy Jenkins, *Gladstone* (London: Macmillan, 1995), p. 403.

3. Fred Halliday, *Islam and the Myth of Confrontation: Religion and Politics in the Middle East* (London: I. B. Tauris, 1999), p. 165.

4. For all this, see Neal Ascherson, *Black Sea: The Birth Place of Civilisation and Barbarism* (London: Vintage, 1996); and Paul Cartledge, *Thermopylae: The Battle That Changed the World* (London: Pan, 2007).

5. Maria Rosa Menocal, *The Ornament of the World: How Muslims, Jews and Christians Created a Culture of Tolerance in Medieval Spain* (New York: Little, Brown, 2002).

6. F. P. Lock, *Edmund Burke*, vol. 2, *1784–1797* (Oxford: Clarendon Press, 2006), pp. 30–31; William Dalrymple, *White Mughals: Love and Betrayal in Eighteenth-Century India* (London: HarperCollins, 2002), passim.

7. Martin Jacques, *When China Rules the World: The Rise of the Middle Kingdom and the End of the Western World* (London: Allen Lane, 2009), pp. 70–71.

8. Angus Maddison, *The World Economy: A Millennial Perspective* (Development Centre of the Organisation for Economic Co-Operation and Development, n.d.), table B-20, p. 263.

9. Amartya Sen, *Identity and Violence* (London: Penguin Books, 2006), pp. 87–88.

10. Thomas Jefferson, letter to Elbridge Gerry, January 26, 1799, Positive Atheism, www.positiveatheism.org/hist/jeff1055.htm; Walt Whitman, "Europe," About.com: Classic Literature, http://classiclit.about.com/library/bl-etexts/wwhitman/bl-ww-europe.htm.

11. The best short account of Europe's condition immediately after the war is in Tony Judt, *Postwar: A History of Europe since 1945* (London: William Heinemann, 2005), chap. 1.

12. Andrew J. Bacevich, ed., *The Imperial Tense: Prospects and Problems of American Empire* (Chicago, Ivan R. Dee, 2003).

13. Bacevich, *Imperial Tense*, p. 73.

14. Robert Kagan, *Paradise and Power: America and Europe in the New World Order* (London: Atlantic Books, 2003), pp. 35–36.

15. "Full Text: Bush's National Security Strategy," September 20, 2002, Common Dreams, http://www.commondreams.org/headlines02/0920-05.htm.

16. The phrase is from Fareed Zakaria, *The Post-American World* (London: Allen Lane, 2008), chap. 1.

17. "Global Trends 2025: A Transformed World," November 2008, National Intelligence Council, www.dni.gov/nic/NIC_2025_project.html.

18. Edmund L. Andrews, "Greenspan Concedes Error on Regulation," *New York Times*, October 23, 2008, http://nytimes.com.

19. Niall Ferguson, *The Ascent of Money: A Financial History of the World* (London: Penguin Books, 2009), p. 230.

20. Quoted in Andrew Gamble, *The Spectre at the Feast: Capitalist Crisis and the Politics of Recession* (Basingstoke: Palgrave Macmillan, 2009), p. 17.

21. For Rehenish capitalism, see Michel Albert, *Capitalisme contre capitalisme* (Paris: Ed. Seuil, 1991); for the banking practices of German banks, see John Lanchester, *Whoops: Why Everyone Owes Everyone and No One can Pay* (London: Allen Lane, 2010), pp. 25–26.

22. Ronnie Chan, "The West's Preaching to the East Must Stop," *Financial Times*, January 4, 2010, p. 13.

23. Zakaria, *Post-American World*, p. 214.

24. Timothy Garton Ash, "Europe Wake Up," *Guardian*, May 20, 2010.

25. Peter Sutherland, "Radical Reforms Can Save the Euro," *Financial Times*, June 30, 2010.

26. Perry Anderson, *The New Old World* (London: Verso, 2009), pp. 47–48.

27. "Global Trends 2025," p. 32.

## 2. Weighing like a Nightmare

1. "Declaration on the Occasion of the Fiftieth Anniversary of the Signature of the Treaties of Rome," EU2007.de, www.eu2007.de/de/News/

download_docs/Maerz/0324-RAA/English.pdf; "Better Institutions for Better Results," March 28, 2007, Europa.eu, http://europa.eu/rapid/press ReleasesAction.do?reference=SPEECH/07/203&.

2. Alistair Horne, *The Price of Glory: Verdun 1916* (London: Penguin, 1993); the French mother's plaque commemorating her son is mentioned on p. xv.

3. For an account of these and other early advocates of a united Europe, see Anderson, *New Old World*, chap. 9.

4. François Duchêne, *Jean Monnet: The First Statesman of Interdependence* (New York: W.W. Norton, 1994), p. 257. See also Alan S. Milward, *The Reconstruction of Western Europe* (London: Methuen, 1984).

5. Duchêne, *Monnet*, p. 188.

6. Alan S. Milward, with the assistance of George Brennan and Frederico Romero, *The European Rescue of the Nation States* (London: Routledge, 1992).

7. Lord Denning, quoted in Anthony Sampson, *Who Runs This Place? The Anatomy of Britain in the 21st Century* (London: John Murray, 2005), p. 367.

8. "How Many Laws from Brussels?" August 3, 2009, www.eulaws .freetzi.com.

9. Lydia, Clapinska, "Post-Legislative Scrutiny of Legislation Derived from the European Union," December 13, 2006, SAS Space E-Repository, Institute of Advanced Legal Studies, http://hdl.handle.net/10065/241.

10. Timothy Snyder, "Holocaust: The Ignored Reality," *New York Review of Books*, July 16, 2009, pp. 14–16.

11. John Barton, "Risen Bodies," *Times Literary Supplement*, no. 5525, February 20, 2009, p. 10.

12. Quoted in Elie Kedourie, *Nationalism*, 4th ed. (Oxford: Blackwell, 1998), p. 125.

13. For a brilliant account of all this, see Michael Mann, *The Dark Side of Democracy: Explaining Ethnic Cleansing* (New York: Cambridge University Press, 2005).

14. Peter Pulzer, *Jews and the German State: The Political History of a Minority* (Oxford: Blackwell, 1992), p. 30.

15. Ian Kershaw, *Hitler, 1936–45: Nemesis*, (London: Allen Lane, 2000), p. 245.

16. Mann, *Dark Side of Democracy*, pp. 185–86.

17. Snyder, "Holocaust."

18. Bernard Wasserstein, *Barbarism and Civilization: A History of Europe in Our Time* (Oxford: Oxford University Press, 2007), p. 401.

19. Wasserstein, *Barbarism*, p. 418; "Expulsion of Germans after World War II," *Wikipedia*, last modified September 13, 2010, http://en .Wikipedia.org/wiki/Expulsion_of_Germans_after_World_War_II.

20. Ireland was assured that it would not be obliged to legalize abortion or to give up its traditional policy of international neutrality. More important, it was also agreed that the Commission would not be slimmed down and that each member state would continue to have one commissioner a piece.

21. Judt, *Postwar*, p. 732.

22. Jean Monnet, *Mémoires* (Paris: Librairies Arthène Fayard, 1976), p. 617.

23. Wolfram Kaiser, *Christian Democracy and the Origins of the European Union* (Cambridge: Cambridge University Press, 2007).

24. Quoted in Edmund Dell, *The Schuman Plan and the British Abdication of Leadership in Europe* (Oxford: Oxford University Press, 1995), p. 16.

25. Duchêne, *Monnet*, p. 235.

26. Walter Hallstein, *Europe in the Making* (London: George Allen and Unwin, 1972), passim, esp. chap. 4.

27. Charles de Gaulle, *Memoirs of Hope: Renewal and Endeavour* (New York: Simon and Schuster, 1971), p. 3.

28. Stephen Wall, *A Stranger in Europe: Britain and the EU from Thatcher to Blair* (Oxford: Oxford University Press, 2008), p. 94.

### 3. HATE—AND HOPE

1. Charles Taylor, "The Politics of Recognition," in *Multiculturalism: A Critical Reader*, ed. David Theo Goldberg (Cambridge, MA: Blackwell, 1994), pp. 75–106.

2. For an interesting account of the "neo-medievalism" of contemporary Europe, see Jan Zielonka, *Europe as Empire: The Nature of the Enlarged European Union* (Oxford: Oxford University Press, 2007), pp. 9–11.

3. Elodie Fabre, "Belgian Federalism in a Comparative Perspective" (Vives Discussion Paper 5, VIVES Vlaams Instituut voor Economie en Samenleving, Research Centre for Regional Economics, July 2009), www.econ .kuleuven.be/vives/PUBLICATIES/DP/DP2009/vivesdiscussionpaper5 .pdf.

4. Marcel Gérard, "Fiscal Federalism in Belgium" (paper presented at the Conference on Fiscal Imbalance, Québec City, Québec, September 13–14, 2001), www.desequilibrefiscal.gouv.qc.ca/en/pdf/gerard.pdf.

5. Eugen Weber, *Peasants into Frenchmen: The Modernization of Rural France, 1870–1914* (London: Chatto and Windus, 1979).

6. Paul M. Heywood, "Spanish Regionalism: A Case Study" (London: Constitution Unit, University College, London, 2000).

7. Robert D. Putnam, *Making Democracy Work: Civic Traditions in Modern Italy* (Princeton, NJ: Princeton University Press, 1993), p. 18.

8. Perry Anderson, "An Entire Order Converted into What It Was Intended to End," *London Review of Books*, February 26, 2009, www.lrb.co.uk/v31/n04/ande01_html.

9. Michele Chang, "Dual Hegemony: France, Germany and the Making of Monetary Union in Europe" (paper prepared for the Biannual Meeting of the European Community Studies Association, Pittsburgh, PA, June 2–5, 1999).

10. Joseph Weiler, quoted in Anthony Giddens, *Europe in the Global Age* (Cambridge, UK: Polity Press, 2007), p. 213.

11. Menon, *Europe: The State of the Union* (London: Atlantic Books, 2008).

12. John Campbell, *Margaret Thatcher*, vol. 2 (London: Pimlico, 2004), p. 303.

13. For the "market state," see Philip Bobbit, *The Shield of Achilles: War, Peace and the Course of History* (London: Penguin, 2003), esp. chap. 10–13.

14. Anthony D. Smith, "National Identity and the Idea of European Unity," *International Affairs* 68, no. 1 (January 1992): 73.

15. "Esther," "Muslim Population in European Cities," *Islam in Europe* (blog), November 23, 2007, http://islamineurope.blogspot.com/2007/11/muslim-population-in-european-cities.html.

16. Malise Ruthven, *A Satanic Affair: Salman Rushdie and the Wrath of Islam* (London: The Hogarth Press, 1991), p. 1.

17. Angelique Chrisafis, "Nicolas Sarkozy Says Islamic Veils Are Not Welcome in France," *Guardian*, June 22, 2009, www.guardian.co.uk.

18. Ian Buruma, *Murder in Amsterdam: The Death of Theo Van Gogh and the Limits of Tolerance* (London: Atlantic Books, 2007); "Theo van Gogh (Film Director)," *Wikipedia*, last modified September 24, 2010, en.wikipedia.org/wiki/Theo_van_Gogh_(film_director).

19. "Jyllands-Posten Muhammad Cartoons Controversy," *Wikipedia*, last modified September 22, 2010, en.wikipedia.org/wiki/Jyllands-Posten_Muhammad_cartoons_controversy.

20. Ibid.

21. For a brilliant autobiographical account of this process, see Ed Husain, *The Islamist: Why I Joined Radical Islam in Britain, What I Saw Inside and Why I Left* (London: Penguin Books, 2007).

22. The term was coined by the novelist and Nobel Prize winner V. S. Naipaul and is quoted in Martin Amis, *The Second Plane: September 11: 2001–2007* (London: Jonathan Cape, 2008), p. 65.

23. Samuel P. Huntington, *The Clash of Civilizations and the Remaking of World Order* (New York: Simon and Schuster, 1996); and Christopher Caldwell, *Reflections on the Revolution in Europe: Immigration, Islam and the West* (London: Allen Lane, 2009).

24. Quoted in Pankaj Misra, "A Culture of Fear," *Guardian*, August 15, 2009, www.guardian.co.uk.

25. Mai Yamani, *Cradle of Islam: The Hijaz and the Quest for an Arabian Identity* (London: I. B. Tauris, 2004).

26. John L. Esposito and Dalia Mogahed, *Who Speaks for Islam: What a Billion Muslims Really Think* (New York: Gallup Press, 2007), chap. 1.

27. Richard Dawkins, *The God Delusion* (London: Bantam Press, 2006); Christopher Hitchens, *God Is Not Great: How Religion Poisons Everything* (New York: Twelve Books, 2007).

28. Mailise Ruthven, *Islam in the World* (Harmondsworth, UK: Penguin Books, 1984), p. 139.

29. Roger Scruton, "The New Humanism," *American Spectator*, March 2009, http://spectator.org.

30. Gertrude Himmelfarb, *Roads to Modernity: The British, French and American Enlightenments* (New York: Alfred A. Knopf, 2004).

31. Menocal, *Ornament of the World*, passim.

## 4. THE REVENGE OF POLITICS

1. Sunil Khilnani, *The Idea of India* (London: Penguin Books, 1999), p. 35.

2. Larry Siedentop, *Democracy in Europe* (London: Allen Lane, 2000).

3. I worked under him in Brussels and regarded him as a political mentor in Britain.

4. Alexander Hamilton, James Madison, and John Jay, "The Federalist no. 22, December 14, 1787," in *The Federalist with The Letters of Brutus*, ed. Terence Ball, Cambridge Texts in the History of Political Thought (Cambridge: Cambridge University Press, 2007), p. 102.

5. See Andrew Moravcsik, *The Choice for Europe: Social Purpose and State Power from Messina to Maastricht*, British ed. (London: UCL Press, 1999), for a critique of "realist" theory and a powerfully argued case for a "liberal intergovernmentalist" alternative theory.

6. Andrew Moravcsik, "Federalism in the European Union: Rhetoric and Reality," in *The Federalist Vision: Legitimacy and Levels of Governance*

*in the United States and the European Union*, ed. Kalypso Nicolaidis and Robert Howse (Oxford: Oxford University Press, 2001), pp. 161–90.

7. Andrew Moravcsik, "Is There a 'Democratic Deficit' in World Politics? A Framework for Analysis," *Government and Opposition* 39, no. 2 (April 2004): 336–63; and Andrew Moravcsik, "Reassessing Legitimacy in the European Union," *Journal of Common Market Studies* 40, no. 4 (2002): 603–24.

8. Mark Leonard, *Why Europe Will Run the 21st Century* (London: Fourth Estate, 2005), pp. 95–98.

9. See my *Parliament for Europe* (London: Jonathan Cape, 1979), pp. 64–66.

10. Maria Misra, *Vishnu's Crowded Temple: India since the Great Rebellion* (London: Penguin Books, 2008), p. 3.

11. Khilnani, *Idea of India*, esp. pp. 34–38.

12. Misra, *Vishnu's Crowded Temple*, pp. 447, 437.

13. Jürgen Habermas, "Toward a Cosmopolitan Europe," *Journal of Democracy* 14 no. 4 (2003): 97–98, quoted in Jan Zielonka, *Europe as Empire: The Nature of the Enlarged European Union* (Oxford: Oxford University Press, 2007), p. 118.

14. For a rich and meaty treatment of the period, see Daniel Howe, *What Hath God Wrought: The Transformation of America* (New York: Oxford University Press, 2007).

15. L. S. Amery, *Thoughts on the Constitution* (Oxford: Oxford University Press, 1964), p. 21.

16. John Dunn, *Setting the People Free: The Story of Democracy* (London: Atlantic Books, 2005), p. 50.

17. Quentin Skinner, "The Italian City-Republics," in *Democracy: The Unfinished Journey, 508 BC to AD 1993*, ed. John Dunn (Oxford: Oxford University Press, 1993), pp. 57–69.

18. Joseph Schumpeter, *Capitalism, Socialism and Democracy* (London: George Allen and Unwin, 1979), p. 267.

19. Schumpeter, *Capitalism, Socialism and Democracy*, p. 268.

20. Philip Pettit, *Republicanism: A Theory of Freedom and Government* (Oxford: Oxford University Press, 1999); and Quentin Skinner, *Liberty before Liberalism* (Cambridge: Cambridge University Press, 1998).

21. Stephen Orgell and Jonathan Goldberg, eds., *John Milton: A Critical Edition of the Major Works* (Oxford: Oxford University Press, 1991), 249–67.

22. Samuel H. Beer, *To Make a Nation: The Rediscovery of American Federalism* (Cambridge, MA: Belknap Press, 1994).

23. "Indian Languages," Maps of India, http://india.mapsofindia.com/the-country/india-forum/indian-languages.html.

5. Which Boundaries? Whose History?

1. Daniel Archibugi and David Held, eds., *Cosmopolitan Democracy: An Agenda for a New World Order* (Cambridge, UK: Polity Press, 1995).

2. Hans Schattle, *The Practices of Global Citizenship* (Lanham, MD: Rowman and Littlefield, 2008).

3. I shall never forget being told by an academic from the former DDR that he wished his West German counterparts didn't give the impression that East Germans had never used forks before reunification.

4. Stefan Zweig, *The World of Yesterday*, trans. Anthea Bell (London: Pushkin Press, 2009), p. 20.

5. Quoted in Jan Zielonka, *Europe as Empire: The Nature of the Enlarged European Union* (Oxford: Oxford University Press, 2007), p. 50. My interpretation of enlargement and the problems associated with it is heavily based on Zielonka's brilliant book.

6. Stephen Wall, *A Stranger in Europe: Britain and the EU from Thatcher to Blair* (Oxford: Oxford University Press, 2008), p. 129; "Chirac Lashes Out at 'New Europe,'" *CNN.com*, February 18, 2003, http://edition .cnn.com/2003/WORLD/europe/02/18/sprj.irq.chirac/.

7. Wall, *Stranger in Europe*, p. 129.

8. Zielonka, *Europe as Empire*, p. 54.

9. I doubt if Donald Rumsfeld, the inventor of the distinction between "New" and "Old" Europe, had this particular division in mind.

10. Samuel P. Huntington, *The Clash of Civilizations and the Remaking of World Order* (New York: Simon and Schuster, 1996).

11. See Leonard, *Why Europe Will Run;* and Zygmunt Bauman, *Europe: An Unfinished Adventure* (Cambridge, UK: Polity Press, 2004).

12. Joseph S. Nye Jr., *The Paradox of American Power: Why the World's Only Superpower Can't Go It Alone* (New York: Oxford University Press, 2002), p. 9.

13. Kagan, *Paradise and Power*, passim.

14. For an illuminating description of patient, bottom-up pluralism in action, see Judith Marquand, *Development Aid in Russia: Lessons from Siberia* (Oxford: Palgrave Macmillan in association with St. Antony's College, 2009).

15. Norman Davies, *Europe: A History* (Oxford: Oxford University Press, 1996), p. xvi.

16. The notion of "patrimonial" rule was invented by Max Weber. See Talcott Parsons, ed., *Max Weber: The Theory of Social and Economic Organization* (New York: Free Press of Glencoe, 1964), pp. 346–54.

17. B. H. Sumner, *Survey of Russian History* (London: Duckworth, 1944), pp. 87–122; and Geoffrey Hosking, *Russia and the Russians: A History from Rus to the Russian Federation* (London: Allen Lane, 2001), pp. 27–127.

18. Fernand Braudel, *A History of Civilizations*, trans. Richard Mayne (New York: Penguin, 1993), p. 22.

19. Menocal, *Ornament of the World*, passim; and Diarmaid Mac-Culloch, *A History of Christianity: The First Three Thousand Years* (London: Allen Lane, 2009), chap. 15.

20. MacCulloch, *History of Christianity*, chap. 11.

21. Judith Herrin, *Byzantium: The Surprising Life of a Medieval Empire*, (London: Penguin Books, 2007), p. 49.

22. Edward Gibbon, *The History of the Decline and Fall of the Roman Empire*, ed. David Womersley (London: Penguin Books, 2000), pp. 437, 439.

23. Alexis de Tocqueville, *Democracy in America* (London: David Campbell, 1994), 2:10, 261.

24. De Tocqueville, *Democracy*, 2:318–19.

25. "Corruption Perceptions Index," *Wikipedia*, last modified September 20, 2010, http://en.wikipedia.org/wiki/Corruption_Perceptions _Index.

26. For this tradition, see Amartya Sen, *The Argumentative Indian: Writings on Indian History and Culture* (London: Allen Lane, 2005).

# INDEX

absolutism, 88, 90–91

accountability: and democratic deficit, 117–18, 123; liberal-individualist, 152

*acquis communitaire* (EU law), 61–62, 149

Adenauer, Konrad, 42, 53, 55–56

Al-Andalus, 100

Albania, 96, 100

Albright, Madeleine, 20

Al Qaeda, 16, 142

Ambedkar, B. R., 104, 105

ambiguity, themes of, in European project, 52–65. *See also specific ambiguities*

American Enlightenment, 99

American federalism. *See* United States, and federalism

Amery, L. S., 125

Andalusia, 74

Anderson, Perry, 75

anti-Semitism: and ethnic nationalism, 38–43, 91, 92, 97; versus medieval Judaeophobia, 37–41

Aristotle, 126, 164, 176

Ashton, Baroness Catherine Margaret, 125

Asia: EU membership eligibility, and geography, 158–59; and Western "honorary members," 9, 12. *See also* China; India; Japan

Asia Minor, 158–59

"assimilation" concept, 97

Atatürk, Kemal, 173–74, 175

Auden, W. H., 123

Austria: accession into EU, 61, 145; and Iraq War, 48; and nationalism, 7, 51;

Pan-European Movement launched by, 30; and World War I, 78, 173

Austria-Hungary land empire, 95, 173

authoritarianism: and "assimilation," 97; and Communism, 115, 150; versus democracy, 157; and pluralism, 171–72

authority: moral, 20, 103, 116; political (*see* political authority)

autistic consumerism, 129, 132, 134

autocracy, 162–63

autonomy, internal, 121

autonomy, political: ethnicity and identity, 69, 71, 73, 74, 76; and identity assumptions, 166

Averroës (Ibn Rushd), 164, 176

balance of power (European), 9, 12

Balkans, 4, 86, 96, 154, 168

Balkan wars, 48

"Ballad of East and West, The" (Kipling), 1, 2, 19, 100, 176

Barroso, José Manuel, 27

Basques, 65, 72, 74

Bear Stearns, 17

Beck, Ulrich, 24

Beer, Samuel, 135

Belarus, 35, 41, 154, 172

Belgium: ethnicity and identity, 55, 72–73; in Europe of the Six, 35; governance and authority, 72–73, 116, 123; and Iraq War, 48; and Islamophobia, 90; and nationalism, 51

189

# INDEX

terrorism, 1, 15–16, 70, 90, 92, 134, 141
Thatcher, Margaret, 14, 47, 50, 56, 57, 81, 108, 152
Thirty Years' War, 53
Thucydides, 102
Tocqueville, Alexis de, 170, 175–76
totalitarianism, 9, 146, 174
trade, EU and, 32, 36, 148
trade tariffs, 32
trade unions, 10, 34, 64
transnationalism, 53
transparency, in decision-making, 23, 133
treaties. *See specific treaty*
Treaty of Westphalia, 53–54, 60, 73, 77–78, 80, 133, 144
tribal democracy, 39, 123, 174, 175
*Triumph of the Will* (Riefenstahl), 39
Trotsky, Leon, 53, 160
Turkey: "Eastern" identity of, historically, 3; ethnic nationalism in, 173–75; and EU enlargement, 154, 164, 173–75; "Western" identity of, post–World War II, 9–10
Turkmenistan, 159
Tymoshenko, Yulia, 172

Ukraine, 41, 154, 172–73, 174, 175
uniformity: and democracy, 118–23; and ethnicity and identity, 72, 121; and India, 121; and "majority will," 118–19; politics of, 72, 74, 121–22, 170; and U.S, 122, 170–71
uniformity and order, politics of, 74
United Kingdom: accession into European Community, 33, 35, 47, 61, 145, 168; British National Party, 51; Conservative Party, 50, 91, 108; devolution statutes, 70; economic crisis of 2007–10, 17–19, 23; electoral system, and democracy, 119; ethnicity and identity, 65, 67–71, 76, 77, 78, 85, 122, 168; and EU Charter

of Fundamental Rights, 103; and EU Constitutional Treaty negotiations, 164; on EU enlargements to the east, 148, 152–53; EU influence on national policy of, 33, 34, 35; and "Europeanism," 144; Euro-skepticism in, 46–47, 50–51; governance and authority, 68–69 (*see also specific parties*); and Iraq War, 48, 129–30; and Islamophobia, 86, 87–88, 91; on Israeli-Palestinian conflict, 40; Labour Party, 50–51, 130; Liberal Democrat Party, 130; on monetary union, 60; and nationalism, 11, 39, 42, 50–51, 138; objections to European federalism in, 138–39; and pluralism, 171; and popular referendum, 33; technocratic rationalism in, 64; Tory Party, 125; and trade unions, 10, 34. *See also constituent countries*
United Kingdom Independence Party (UKIP), 50
United Kingdom Parliament, 68
United Nations climate change conference (Copenhagen, 2009), 17, 20
United Nations Security Council, 77
United States: American Revolution, 122, 132, 135–36; challenges to moral authority of, 20; challenges to political authority of, 20–21; as "city on a hill," 1, 15, 21, 24, 176; Civil War, 120, 126, 130–31, 132, 142; class, and democracy in, 129; and cold war, 9, 10, 12, 14, 15, 29; economic crisis of 2007, 17–20; economic projection (2025), 16; and evolution of civilization, 166; and federalism, 66, 105, 112, 135–37, 138; "high" versus "low" politics in, 107, 108; historically isolationist policy of, 7–8; and identity, 161; and Iraq War, 15–16, 48, 83, 125, 129–30;

203

The Public Square Book Series
Princeton University Press

With Thanks to the Donors of the Public Square

President William P. Kelly, the CUNY Graduate Center
Myron S. Glucksman
Caroline Urvater